Capron and Johnson's

Pocket Internet

4001 SITES

H. L. CAPRON
J. A. JOHNSON

Pearson Education

Prentice Hall
Upper Saddle River,
New Jersey 07458

Prentice-Hall International (UK) Limited, London
Prentice-Hall of Australia Pty. Limited, Sydney
Prentice-Hall Canada, Inc., Toronto
Prentice-Hall Hispanoamericana, S.A., Mexico
Prentice-Hall of India Private Limited, New Delhi
Prentice-Hall of Japan, Inc., Tokyo
Pearson Education Asia Pte. Ltd., Singapore
Editora Prentice-Hall do Brasil, Ltda., Rio de Janerio

ISBN   0-13-091956-X

Printed in the United States of America.
* 2 3 4 5 6 7 8 9 10*

POCKET START

How much do I need to know in order to use the Internet?

Not much. That is a good part of the reason for its popularity. The best way to get started is to have someone give you a demonstration. When you see how easy it is, you will want to begin clicking and linking on your own.

Clicking and linking?

Yes. Use a mouse to click on a bit of colored text or a small image—the link—and you will be transferred to the Web site—on another computer—that the link represents. The World Wide Web, an Internet subset usually referred to as "the Web," is a collection of Web sites with information from other computers that you can see on your own computer screen. Once you get started, you can indeed just click-and-link from site to site. The total set of links is seen as a giant spider's web, hence the name "the Web."

You said "once you get started." How does that happen?

If you are in a computer-equipped environment—a school, a library, a workplace—the hardware and software to access the Internet are probably already in place. If you want to access the Internet from your own personal computer, the only other hardware you need is a modem so that you can make a physical com-

munications link via your telephone system.
Besides the modem software (which usually
comes installed on the computer) the main software that you need for your own computer is
called a browser, because you will be using it to
browse the Internet. But you will also need
access to another computer called a server. You
could think of the server as sort of a gateway; it
has the software that makes the actual connection to the Internet. Once all these items are in
place, you use the browser to contact the server
via the modem and the phone system. You will
see a Web site on your screen, usually the site
for the browser's manufacturer or a site you
have chosen to see everytime you open the
browser. It will have the links we mentioned,
the colored text or images, and now you can
begin—clicking and linking.

That's it?
That really is it, except that we left out most of
the buzzwords. And we should also mention that
there is not just one server, but tens of thousands. You have to get access to one of them to
get online. You can look for a local Internet service provider (ISP) in your area and sign up to
use its servers, usually for a monthly fee. The
ISP will tell you how to configure your browser
or other software to connect to their servers. On
the other hand, you might do what many people
do—sign up for an online service such as
America Online and let them worry about the
server. Most ISPs have several servers; they may
use one or more for a mail server, another for

usenet, others for customers web sites, etc, Also, many individuals and companies have their own servers. A server is a computer, the term server is not a synonym for service provider.

And the buzzwords?

Just so you have seen the correct terminology, we will describe the whole setup in formal terms. "Internet" means, literally, a network of networks. You will use a browser to click on hypertext, the kind of text that operates as a link because it represents a Uniform Resource Locator (URL), the address of the Web site. You can see the URL of the current site in the long, skinny window—the address slot—near the top of the browser; the URL changes when you link to a new site. A server is a computer, often (but not always) operated by an Internet service provider (ISP), and servers that you will use to access Web sites use software called Transmission Control Protocol/Internet Protocol (TCP/IP) to access the Internet and route files. Web site pages are written in a language called Hyper - Text Markup Language (HTML). The main page of a Web site is referred to as its home page. You can use a scroll bar to move up and down the pages of the site. You can click browser buttons to move Back to the previous site or Forward again or to Print or Reload the page.

I think I need to see a demonstration.

Good idea.

Add just a bit of history, and you will know as much about the Internet as most casual users. The Internet began in 1969 as ARPANet, sponsored by the U.S. Department of Defense to connect widely scattered computers so that no one nuclear bomb could wipe out our computing and communication capabilities. As Cold War fears receded and computer networks spread, the network became more public, more generic, and more commercial—and took the new name "Internet."

The World Wide Web was conceived by a fellow named Tim Berners-Lee, who was working in a particle physics lab called CERN in Geneva, Switzerland. He thought it would be convenient if he could just link to the computers of his fellow physicists around the world, so he proceeded to set up the first web. The other major development was the graphical browser, invented by Marc Andreessen, which made possible the easy clicking and linking. That's the bare-bones history.

One more thing. How do I access a Web site I've heard about?

If you know the URL (for example, http://www.nike.com), you can type it in your browser's address slot and press Enter. In this example, you will be transported to the Nike site. Of course, you are not really going anywhere; it only seems that way. In truth, your browser sends a message to contact the Nike site, and Nike sends its files (via several servers and finally to your ISP's server) to your computer.

If you know only the subject matter (say, the name Nike) but not the URL, you can submit the name to a site that runs software called a search engine, which finds sites that match the given name. Search engines are not limited to a name; you could give it several terms, such as "athletic apparel," and it would return a list of sites matching the terms. The listed sites are presented as links, so you need only click on a link name to be transported to the chosen site. Several search engines are listed in this book, among site listings, under the heading Internet Search Engines.

Most people soon establish favorite sites and return to them again and again to see what's new and to follow new links from there. Your browser will let you save the addresses of such sites in a list by clicking a button called Favorites, Bookmarks, or something similar; when you want to visit that site again, you can then simply click on the saved link rather than having to retype the site's address.

Is there a table of contents or an index for the Internet?

Not exactly. No one owns the Internet, nor is anyone actually in charge of it. Several organizations attempt to organize the Internet, producing directories or catalogs. Several are listed in this book, under the heading Internet Directories. Although none of them would claim to be exhaustive, they offer the Internet in their own way. Any one of them would be a nice place to start.

▌ POCKET FAQs

What is a FAQ?

The term "FAQ" is an abbreviation for "frequently asked question." Most beginners have similar questions, so experienced users compile FAQs to be helpful to newcomers. You can get answers before you have even thought of the questions.

How many people are connected to the Internet?

In the United States, about 35 to 40 million households have computers, and about half of them have modems and some sort of connection to the Internet. These numbers should double by the year 2002. Many more users access the Internet from their workplaces.

Are most users businesspeople? Men? Teenagers?

Studies show many business users, but they are not the majority. More men than women are on the Internet, but the gap is closing quickly. Users tend to be youngish but, generally, not teen-agers. Most users tend to be in their late twenties or early thirties. A more distinct trend is that Internet users tend to be rather well educated (about half have a college degree) and rather well-off—middle-class or above.

It's called the World Wide Web, but isn't it mostly in the United States?

Yes and no. There is a higher percentage of Web users in the United States than in other countries, but there are many, many users around the world, in more than 100 different countries, easily enough to make the term "World Wide Web" meaningful.

Why is the Internet so popular?

The Internet offers an extraordinary amount of information on just about any topic. But so does a library. The difference is accessibility. The simple click-on-a-link user interface is attractive to both novices and sophisticated users. What is more, you can click and link right in your own home, at any time of the day or night, wearing your bathrobe if you wish. In addition to being a resource of information, the Internet notches up the convenience level for many services—You need make only a few clicks to check your mutual fund, order tickets, or send flowers. Add to this the attractiveness of the graphics, the cleverness of the offerings, and the—mostly—reasonable cost of participation, and the package is hard to resist.

What are people doing on the Internet?

Many people are gathering information—for reports, for term papers, for businesses, for hobbies, and much more. Some people do a fair amount of shopping, especially for books and music and occasionally for last-minute gifts that can be sent directly to the recipient. Some are playing games or participating in chat rooms and other types of cyberspace communities. But the vast majority are surfing—just clicking from site to site to see what they happen to encounter.

▼ POCKET TIPS

My browser looks pretty ordinary, mostly gray.
The default browser look is "plain vanilla," but you can use the preferences menu on your browser to change the colors of the links, the followed links (ones you have already visited), and the background. You can also change the look and size of the font and even the language.

Anything else?
You can set e-mail and security options to suit your convenience, and you can even change the home page that comes up when you use the browser to access the Internet. Under the browser's Help menu, you can find extensive information about how the browser works and how to configure it. But keep in mind that these are options; the browser works just fine if you do none of these things.

I usually enjoy the visual aspects of a site, but sometimes I am just looking for specific information and get tired of waiting for all the fancy graphics to load.
Check your browser's options list. You can control whether images are automatically downloaded with the site; that is, you can specify text only. This will speed up site loading significantly. You can, of course, go back to including graphics whenever you wish. Also, many sites include a text-only link on the opening page.

I am worried about catching a virus from the Internet.

First, your computer cannot catch a virus if you are just looking. Surfing from one Web site to another is perfectly safe. You can even safely fill out forms or supply information in other ways if you wish. However, your computer can catch a virus if you download a program from a Web site, or any place else on the Internet, and execute it. Although it is generally safe to download software from major vendors, you are taking a risk if you use software from an unknown—and thus unreliable—source.

Just how safe is it to give out my credit card number to make a purchase from a Web site?

At this point, probably no one would guarantee across-the-board safety. However, several well-known vendor sites encrypt (scramble, so that it is unreadable by others) the data you send from your computer to theirs, and they are willing to guarantee its security. If you feel uneasy about this, you can get product information from the site and use your telephone to place the order by voice.

I see counters on several sites but not on the more sophisticated commercial sites. Don't they care how many people visit their sites?

They care, all right. But they want much more information than can be provided by a simple counter, which merely records the number of visits, not even the number of visitors. A number of software packages are available to monitor a Web site, providing such statistics as usage by domain and country, the parts of the site visited, and the peak hours of access to the site. All of this, of course, is done without the site visitor being aware of it. Most important, the software can also determine from what site you have just come. This information can, among other things, reveal the sites where clickable advertising banners are most effective.

I see some great looking images on Web sites that I'd like to have and maybe even use on my own home page. How can I get them?

There are several ways to capture images that you see on the screen. But first, note that you cannot help yourself to just any image on the screen; to do so could be a copyright infringement. But some images have been made freely available.

The easiest capture method, if you have a browser such as Netscape or Internet Explorer, is to rest the mouse over the desired image and click the right mouse button. This will cause a menu to appear. Now click the left mouse button on the Save option and choose a directory and name for the file. If you want to capture an entire screen, one that probably has several images, you can use screen capture software.

I know a little about HTML and would like to study how some of the sites I view were written.

Most browsers have an option called View Source. Simply click it, and the HTML source code for the current site will show on the screen.

How can I find out someone's e-mail address?

First, don't bother trying to find the private e-mail address of a celebrity. Their addresses are no more available than their telephone numbers. If you want the e-mail address of someone you know, the most straightforward—and probably fastest—way is to ask the person. Some online services will let you, as a member, look up other members by name, but success depends on whether the other person is a member and, if so, whether he or she has filed something akin to a member profile. You can try submitting the person's name to a search engine; a site that carries the person's name might also point to an e-mail address or to someone else who might have it. Some sites, notably WhoWhere and Switchboard, perform e-mail address searches. It should be noted that if the person guards his or her e-mail address, it is unlikely that any of these approaches will work.

How can I get rid of junk e-mail?

Junk e-mail is one of the toughest issues on the Internet, and there are no definitive answers. The easiest way to avoid it is the same way you avoid ordinary junk mail or junk telephone calls: Hide. If you do not reveal your home address or phone number casually, then you understand that you don't give your e-mail address out casually either. Prevention is the best cure. Bear in mind that each place you leave your e-mail address—chat rooms, Web vendors, newsgroups, contests, and so on—is one more place from which your e-mail address can be harvested and sold by others.

Once the junk mail starts coming in, you can attempt to stem the tide in various ways. The obvious approach is to tell the sender to remove you from the mailing list. This may work for responsible companies. You can probably report the offending sender's e-mail address and, given sufficient complaint volume, the service might cut off that sender's access. But don't count on it. A high-volume sender has probably already moved on. If you belong to an online service such as America Online, find out what measures the service takes to reduce junk mail for its members. Many ISPs also offer easy-to-use e-mail filters. Finally, you can buy your own filter software to control from which e-mail addresses you will accept messages.

POCKET DICTIONARY

Applet A small program that can provide animation such as dancing icons and scrolling banners on a Web site.

ARPANet The network established in 1969 by the Department of Defense that eventually became the Internet.

Authoring Software Software that lets a user make a Web page without having knowledge of HTML; the software covers specifications to HTML.

Backbone The major communications links that tie Internet servers across wide geographical areas.

Background On a Web site, the screen appearance behind the text and images. A background is often a plain color, a color with some texture to it, or perhaps an image or set of images.

Bandwidth The number of frequencies that can fit on one communications line or link at the same time, or the capacity of the communications link.

Banner Ad A Web site advertisement, often in the shape of a rectangle, that, when clicked, sends the user to the advertised site, called an affiliate. A live banner lets a user get more information about a product without leaving the current site.

Boolean logic A mathematical system that many search engines can use to narrow the search by using operators such as AND, OR, and NOT.

Browser Software that is used to access the Internet.

CERN The name of the site of the particle physics lab where Dr. Tim Berners-Lee worked when he invented the World Wide Web; sometimes considered the birthplace of the Web.

Cookie A file stored on the user's hard drive that reflects activity on the Internet. For example, a site that sells a product or service may record a cookie indicating what parts of the site a user visited and, on the basis of this, may guide the user or offer certain services on subsequent visits.

Clickable image Any image that has instructions embedded in it so that clicking on it initiates some kind of action or result, usually transferring to another site or another location within the same site. Also called a hyperregion.

Clickthrough A reference to users who leave the current Internet site for a site that is advertised on the current site

Contextsensitive A reference to Web advertisements that are related to the subject matter on the screen.

Cyberspace A term coined by science fiction author William Gibson, now used to describe the whole range of information resources available through computer networks.

Data compression Making a large data file smaller by temporarily removing nonessential but space-hogging items such as tab marks and double-spacing. Compressed files take up less space on a server or hard drive and travel faster over a network.

Domain name The unique name that identifies the address of an Internet site. The Internet is made up of hundreds of thousands of computers and networks; each site has its own domain name or unique address. Domain names always have two or more parts separated by dots, for example, netscape.com.

Download In a networking environment, receiving data files from another computer, probably a larger computer or a server. Contrast with *Upload.*

Digital subscriber line (DSL) A service that uses advanced electronics to send data over conventional copper telephone wires at much higher rates than is possible with regular modems.

E-mail (electronic mail) Sending messages from one computer to another.

Extranet A network of two or more intranets.

FAQ The acronym for "frequently asked questions." FAQs are online documents that list and answer the most common questions on a particular subject.

Firewall A dedicated computer with the sole purpose of talking to the outside world and deciding who gains entry to a company's private network or intranet.

Flaming Sending insulting e-mail, chat, or Usenet messages, often by large numbers of people in response to spamming. A flame war occurs when two or more users flame each other in an escalating manner that threatens to continue unabated.

Frames The capability of some browsers to display pages of a site in separate sections, each of which may operate independently.

FTP A set of rules for transferring files from one computer to another. Most browsers support using FTP by typing the URL in the browser's location slot. For example: ftp://site.xxx/directory/filexxx.yyy will transfer filexxx.yyy from site.xxx to your computer's hard disk.

GIF The acronym for "Graphics Interchange Format," a graphics file format that compresses files so that they can be transmitted quickly over a network. GIF is the most commonly used graphics format on the World Wide Web, though it is a proprietary format that was not intended to be used so freely. It is gradually being superseded by a format known as Portable Network Graphics, which has the extension PNG.

Gopher An Internet subsystem that lets a user find files through a series of narrowing menus.

Graphical user interface (GUI) An image-based computer interface in which the user sends directions to the operating system by selecting icons from a menu or manipulating icons on the screen by using a pointing device such as a mouse.

Home page The main page of a Web site.

Hot list A list of names and URLs of favorite Web sites. Most browsers support hot lists, called bookmarks, favorites, or something similar. Once a site is placed on the hot list, a user can access it quickly by clicking on its name.

HTML See *Hypertext Markup Language.*

HTTP See *HyperText Transfer Protocol.*

Hyperregion An icon or image that can be clicked to cause a link to another Web site. Also called a *clickable image.*

Hypertext Text that can be clicked to cause a link to another Web site; hypertext is usu-ally distinguished by a different color and perhaps underlining.

Hyptertext Markup Language (HTML) A programming language used to write documents containing hypertext, in particular, pages for the Web.

HyperText Transfer Protocol (HTTP) A set of rules that provide the means of communicating on the World Wide Web by using links. Note the *http* as the beginning of each Web address.

Icon A small picture on a computer screen; it represents a computer activity.

Image map A graphic that is divided so that when a particular region is clicked, it calls up a Web page associated with that particular region. On a site offering national information such as weather, for example, clicking on a particular state on an image map of the United States calls up the appropriate page for that state.

Inline image In HTML, an image that is referenced right in the HTML code and whose files are loaded with the HTML code. The image is displayed on the same page as the text.

Internet A public communications network that was once used primarily by businesses, governments, and academic institutions but now is also used by individuals via various private access methods.

Internet service provider (ISP) A company that offers, for a fee, access to one or more server computers and the software needed to access the Internet.

Intranet A private Internet-like network that is internal to a certain company.

ISP See *Internet service provider.*

Java A network-friendly programming language, derived from the C++ language, that allows software to run on many different platforms. In particular, Java is used to write small animations called *applets.*

JPEG The acronym for "Joint Photographic Experts Group," an industry committee that developed a compression standard for still images. JPEG refers to the graphics file format that uses this compression standard. JPEG files on the Web have the file extension JPG.

Lurking Reading messages in newsgroups or chat rooms without writing any.

MIME The acronym for "Multipurpose Internet Mail Extension," an Internet protocol that allows users to send binary files across the Internet as attachments to e-mail messages. This includes graphics, photos, sound and video files, and formatted text documents.

Mirror A site that is identical to another site, that is, it offers an alternative way to access the same files. A mirror site is used when a site is so popular that the volume of users accessing it keeps others from getting through or to make the material available closer to the user's geographic location.

MPEG The acronym for "motion picture experts group," a set of widely accepted digital video and audio standards.

Multimedia Software that typically presents information with text, illustrations, photos, narration, music, animation, and film clips.

Netiquette An informal code of appropriate behavior in network communications.

Newsgroup An online discussion forum that focuses on a specific topic. A newsgroup is much like a virtual bulletin board where anyone may post a message and read or respond to messages that others have posted. Some, but not all, newsgroups are part of a system called Usenet.

Packet A portion of a message to be sent to another computer via data communications. Each packet is individually addressed. The packet may take different routes and are reassembled into the original message once they reach their destination.

Plug-in Software that can be added to a browser to enhance its functionality.

Push technology Software that automatically sends—pushes—information from the Internet to a user's personal computer. Also called *webcasting*.

Search engine Software that lets a user specify search terms that can be used to find Web sites that include those terms. The search engine provides a list of the results in hypertext, which means that a user can click on any item in the list to go to that site.

Server A computer that is used to access the Internet; it has special software that uses the Internet protocol.

Shockwave A set of programs that can be added to a browser as a plug-in, allowing the browser to present animated files. Typical applications of Shockwave are games, animated logos, and advertising.

Spamming Mass advertising on the Internet, usually by using software especially designed to send solicitations to users via e-mail.

Tag In HTML, a command that performs a specific function.

TCP/IP See *Transmission Control Protocol/ Internet Protocol.*

Tile In reference to a screen background, particularly on a Web site, spreading a pattern down and across the screen to make a complete background.

Transmission Control Protocol/Internet Protocol (TCP/IP) A standardized protocol permitting different computers to communicate via the Internet.

Uniform Resource Locator (URL) The unique address of a Web page or other file on the Internet.

Upload In a networking environment, sending a file from one computer to another, usually to a larger computer or a host computer. Con-trast with *Download.*

URL See *Uniform Resource Locator.*

Usenet A loosely networked collection of computers around the world that allow the posting and reading of messages in newsgroups that focus on specific topics. See also *newsgroups.*

Web See *World Wide Web.*

Web site An individual location on the World Wide Web.

Webcasting Software that automatically sends—pushes—information from the Internet to a user's personal computer. Also called *push technology.*

Webmaster The administrator responsible for the management and often the design of a World Wide Web site.

World Wide Web (WWW or the Web) An Internet subset of sites with text, images, and sounds; most Web sites provide links to related topics.

4001 SITES

Accounting

If it is true that an accounting major's main concern is the CPA exam, then there is help here. There are also a number of sites for the accounting professional. See also Taxes.

❏ **Accountant's Home Page**
www.computercpa.com/

❏ **Accounting Professionals' Resource Center**
www.kentis.com/

❏ **Electronic Accountant**
www.electronicaccountant.com

❏ **How to Apply for the CPA Exam**
www.wiseguides.com/cpabds.htm

❏ **Pro2Net**
www.pro2net.com/

❏ **European Accounting Association**
www.bham.ac.uk/EAA/

❏ **Careers in Accounting**
www.careers-in-accounting.com/

❏ **General Accounting Office**
w3.access.gpo.gov/gao/

❏ **Accounting Web Sites**
acct.tamu.edu/smith/acctwebs.htm

Agriculture

There is much serious stuff in this list, mostly from the government or other organizations.

❏ **Agribiz**
www.agribiz.com/

❏ **Agriculture Committee of the U.S. House of Representatives**
agriculture.house.gov/

❏ **Agriculture Economics Journals**
www.sciencekomm.at/journals/economic.html

❏ **Agriculture Online**
www.agriculture.com/

❏ **Agriculture Virtual Library**
www.vlib.org/Agriculture.html

❏ **AgriSurf**
www.agrisurf.com/

❏ **Alliance for Sustainability**
www.mtn.org/iasa/

❏ **American Crop Protection Association**
www.acpa.org/

❏ **Community Supported Agriculture (CSA) Farms by State**
www.biodynamics.com/usda/

❏ **Cybersteed**
www.cybersteed.com/

❏ **Dairy Network**
www.dairynetwork.com/

❏ **Department of Agriculture**
www.usda.gov/

❏ **Farm and Ranch Business Center**
www.traderivers.com/farmranch/index.html

❏ **Fruit Facts**
www.crfg.org/pubs/frtfacts.html

❏ **Grain Net**
www.grainnet.com/BreakingNews/index.html

❏ **HayNet**
www.dairynetwork.com/

❏ **Homefarm**
www.traderivers.com/farmranch/index.html

❏ **House Committee on Agriculture**
www.house.gov/agriculture/

❏ **Moo Milk**
www.moomilk.com/

❏ **National Agricultural Statistics Service**
www.usda.gov/nass/

❏ **Seeds of Life**
versicolores.ca/SeedsOfLife/

❏ **Small Farm Resource**
www.farminfo.org/

❏ **Sustainable Agriculture Network**
www.sare.org/

❏ **The Coop**
www.the-coop.org/index.html

❏ **The Eggman**
www.hughson.com/eggman/

❏ **Urban Agriculture Notes**
www.cityfarmer.org/

❏ **USDA-NASS Census of Agriculture**
www.nass.usda.gov/census/census92/
agrimenu.htm

❏ **USDA-Natural Resources Conservation Service**
www.ncg.nrcs.usda.gov/

❏ **World Sustainable Agriculture Association**
www.igc.org/wsaala/

Animals and Birds

The sites in this list provide information to help you care for your domestic pet. And there are a few sites for nondomestic animals and birds.

❏ **American Kennel Club**
www.akc.org/

❏ **American Rare Breed Association**
www.arba.org/

❏ **Birding on the Web**
www-stat.wharton.upenn.edu/~siler.birding.
html

❏ **Birds.com**
www.birds.com/

❏ **Birds of Prey**
www.buteo.com/

❏ **Care for Pets**
www.avma.org/care4pets/default.htm

❏ **Cat Fanciers**
www.fanciers.com/

❏ **CyberPet**
www.cyberpet.com/

❏ **Cybersteed**
www.cybersteed.com/

❏ **Doggy Information**
www.bulldog.org/dogs/

❏ **Dogs and Horses: Breeds and Colours**
www.tekstotaal.com/crasfarb.html

❏ **FatCat**
www.fatcats.com/

❏ **House Rabbit**
www.rabbit.org/

❏ **Hummingbirds**
www.derived.net/hummers/

❏ **Humming Birds**
members.aol.com/wckdlalady/hummers.htm

❏ **Kitten Rescue**
www.kittenrescue.org/

❏ **Mammals of Everglades National Park**
www.nps.gov/ever/ed/edmammal.htm

❏ **Mammals of the Ice**
rimmer.design1.com.au/mammals/

❏ **National Audubon Society**
www.audubon.org/

❏ **Nestbox**
www.nestbox.com/

❏ **NetVet**
netvet.wustl.edu/

❏ **Oriental Birds**
www.orintalbirdclub.org/

❏ **Painted Horses Webring**
www.paint-horse.com/paintedhorses/

❏ **Pet Channel**
www.thepetchannel.com/

❏ **Petz Central**
www.petz.com/

❏ **Pet Loss, Bereavement, Memorials,
Tributes and Support**
www.in-memory-of-pets.com/

❏ **Rainforest Mammals**
kids.osd.wednet.edu/Marshall/homepage/
mammals.html

❏ **South Florida Birding**
www.southfloridabirding.com/index.htm

❏ **State Birds**
www.50states.com/bird/

❏ **Tame Beast**
www.tamebeast.com/

❏ **The Birds of North America**
www.birdsofna.org/

❏ **Travel Dog**
www.traveldog.com/

Architecture

There are fewer architecture sites than you might expect, but the ones that do exist have rich content and are well worth a visit.

❏ **Ace Architects**
www.aceland.com/

❏ **AEC InfoCenter**
www.aecinfo.com/

❏ **American Institute of Architecture Students**
www.aiasnatl.org/

❏ **American Institute of Architects**
www.aecinfo.com/

❏ **Ancient City of Athens**
www.indiana.edu/~kglowack/Athens/Athens
.html

❏ **ArchE+/BBZine**
www.usaor.net/users/archeplus/BBZine.html

❏ **ArchINFORM**
www.archinform.de/

❏ **Architecture Magazine**
www.architecturemag.com/

❑ **Architects, Engineers, Contractors**
www.aecinfo.com/

❑ **Architecture and Building Links**
www.architecturelinks.com/

❑ **Barn Journal**
Musueum.cl.msu.edu/barn/

❑ **Buckminster Fuller**
www.pbs.org/wnet/bucky.cgi

❑ **Cyburbia**
www.arch.buffalo.edu/pairc/

❑ **Frank Lloyd Wright**
www.mcs.com/~tgiesler/flw_home.htm#links

❑ **Frank Lloyd Wright Foundation**
www.franklloydwright.org/

❑ **Hillier Group**
www.hillier.com/

❑ **Irish Architecture Online**
www.archeire.com/

❑ **Jones and Jones**
www.jonesandjones.com

❑ **Lundstrom**
www.lundstromarch.com/

❑ **Medieval Art and Architecture**
www1.pitt.edu/~medart/index.html

❑ **New York Architecture Images**
members.nbci.com/iNetwork/NYC_Images/
imgentry.html

❑ **Plan Net**
www.plannet.com/

Artificial Intelligence

Artificial intelligence could be considered the high end of computer science. Many of these sites contain sophisticated content.

❑ **Artificial Intelligence Center**
www.ai.sri.com/

❑ **Artificial Intelligence FAQ: AI Web Directories**
www.landfield.com/faqs/ai-faq/general/part5/

❑ **Artificial Intelligence and Games**
www.brl.ntt.co.jp/people/kojima/links/ai-game.html

❑ **Artificial Intelligence Group—JPL**
www-aig.jpl.nasa.gov/

❑ **Artificial Intelligence Introduction**
tqd.advanced.org/2705/

❑ **Artificial Intelligence Library**
www.cs.reading.ac.uk/people/dwc/ai.html

❑ **Artificial Intelligence Resources**
Ai.iit.nrc.ca/ai_point.html

❑ **Artificial Intelligence Tools**
www.wspc.com/journals/ijait/ijait.html

❑ **Context in Artificial Intelligence**
tqd.Advanced.org/2705/

❏ **Evaluation of Intelligent Systems**
eksl-www.cs.umass.edu/eis/

❏ **Game AI**
www.gameai.com/ai.html

❏ **Japanese Society for Artificial Intelligence**
www.soc.nacsis.ac.jp/jsai/

❏ **Journal of Artificial Intelligence Systems**
www.brunel.ac.uk/~hssrjis/

❏ **MIT Artificial Intelligence Lab**
Libraries.mit.edu/docs/

❏ **Stanford Knowledge Systems Lab**
www-ksl.stanford.edu/

Arts

Galleries, art departments, and individual artists are featured here.

❏ **Agent 13**
Agent13.com/

❏ **Ankiewicz Galleries**
www.ankiewicz.com

❏ **Art Crimes**
artcrimes.gatech.edu

❏ **Art of the First World War**
www.art-ww1.com/gb/index2.html

❏ **Art of Tibet**
www.tibetart.com/

❏ **ArtDaily**
www.artdaily.com/

❏ **Arts**
www.awa.com/arts.html

❏ **Art.com**
www.art.com/

❏ **Arts Wire**
artswire.org/

❏ **Asian Arts**
www.webart.com/asianart/index.html

❏ **Babel**
www.babelny.com/

❏ **Chicago Museum of Contemporary Art**
www.mcachicago.org/

❏ **Dale Chihuly**
www.chihuly.com/

❏ **Doubletake Gallery**
www.DoubletakeArt.com/

❏ **Electric Art Gallery**
www.egallery.com/

❏ **EroticArt.com**
www.tantra-sex.com/art.html

❏ **Gallery Online**
www.galleryonline.com/

❏ **Gustav Klimt Art Gallery**
www.magma.ca/~alexxi/klimt/1klimt.htm

❏ **Hackett-Freedman Online Gallery**
www.realart.com/

❏ **Incredible Art Department**
www.artswire.org/kenroar/

❏ **Lounge Gallery of Art**
www.the-lounge.com/

❏ **Martin Lawrence Galleries**
www.martinlawrence.com/

❏ **Mundo das Artes**
www.interart.com.br/

❏ **Musees de Paris**
www.paris.org/Musees/

❏ **Museum of Bad Art**
Glyphs.com/moba/

❏ **MOCA: The Museum of Computer Art**
www.museumofcomputerart.com/

❏ **MoMA: The Museum of Modern Art,
New York**
www.moma.org/

❏ **National Endowment for the Arts**
arts.endow.gov/

❏ **National Gallery of Art**
www.nga.gov/

❏ **New Chinese Art**
www.asiasociety.org/arts/insideout/

❏ **On the Road in China**
www.zama.com/ontheroad/

❑ **Orange Show**
www.insync.net/~orange/

❑ **Portraits in Cyberspsace**
persona.www.media.mit.edu/1010/Exhibit/

❑ **Remedi Project**
www.theremediproject.com/

❑ **Salvador Dali Collection**
www.webcoast.com/Dali/collection.htm

❑ **SevenSeven**
www.sevenseven.com/

❑ **Van Gogh Gallery**
www.vangoghgallery.com/

❑ **Walker Art Center**
www.walkerart.org/

❑ **Web Art**
www.mowa.org/

Astronomy

Mostly formal astronomy study.

❑ **American Astronomical Society**
www.aas.org/

❑ **Astronomy Picture of the Day**
Antwrp.gsfc.nasa.gov/apod/astropix.html

❑ **AstroWeb Consortium**
www.cv.nrao.edu/fits/www/astroweb.html

❑ **Cambridge Astronomy**
www.ast.cam.ac.uk/

❑ **Comets and Meteor Showers**
comets.amsmeteors.org/

❑ **Earth and Sky**
www.earthsky.com/

❑ **Earth Viewer**
www.fourmilab.ch/earthview/vplanet.html

❑ **Greek Astronomy**
www.ibiblio.org/expo/vatican.exhibit/
exhibit/d-mathematics/Greek_astro.html

❑ **Griffith Observatory**
www.griffithobs.org/

❑ **Images of Galaxies**
Zebu.uoregon.edu/galaxy.html

❑ **Inconstant Moon**
www.inconstantmoon.com/

❑ **Popular Astronomy Magazine**
www.popastro.com/spapop/home.htm

❑ **Should We Return to the Moon?**
www.ari.net/back2moon.html

❑ **Sky and Telescope Magazine**
www.skypub.com/

❑ **The Maya Astronomy Page**
www.michielb.nl/maya/astro.html

❑ **U.S. Naval Observatory**
www.usno.naavy.mil/

❑ **University of Massachusetts Astronomy Department**
donald.phast.umass.edu/

❑ **University of Washington Astronomy Department**
www.astro.washington.edu/

❑ **Web Nebulae**
seds.lpl.arizona.edu/billa/twn/top.html

❑ **Windows to the Universe**
www.windows.umich.edu/

Auctions

Most of the sites listed here are for online auctions—List, sell, bid, and buy right from your computer at home. A few sites describe land-based auctions.

❑ **Auction! Auction!**
Auctionauction.com/

❑ **Auction Depot**
www.auctiondepot.com/

❑ **Auction Guide**
www.auctionguide.com/index.htm

❑ **Auction Hunter**
www.auctionhunter.com/

❑ **Auction Patrol**
www.auctionpatrol.com/

❑ **Auction Watch**
www.auctionwatch.com/

❑ **AuctionBiz**
www.auctionbiz.com/

❏ **BidMore Online Internet Auction**
www.bidmore.com/

❏ **BidNow**
www.bidnow.com/

❏ **Buffalo Bid Antique Auction**
www.buffalobid.com/

❏ **Buy Collectibles**
www.buycollectibles.com/

❏ **Christie's**
www.christies.com/

❏ **Collector Online**
www.collectoronline.com/

❏ **Cyberswap**
www.cyberswap.com/

❏ **DealDeal**
www.dealdeal.com/

❏ **eBay**
www.ebay.com/

❏ **EZbid**
www.ezbid.com/

❏ **First Auction**
www.firstauction.com/

❏ **Global Auction**
Global-auction.com/

❏ **Guitar Auction**
www.guitarauction.com/

❏ **Interactive Collector**
www.icollector.com/

❏ **Internet Auction List**
www.internetauctionlist.com/

❏ **Online Auction**
www.online-auction.com/

❏ **Online Auction Users Association**
www.auctionusers.org/

❏ **OnSale Computer Auction**
www.onsale.com/

❏ **Pottery Auction**
www.potteryauction.com/

❏ **Sotheby's**
www.sothebys.com/

❏ **Sporting Auction**
www.sportingauction.com/

❏ **The World's Best New Age Auction**
www.newageauction.com/

❏ **uBid**
www.ubid.com/

❏ **Vintage Poster Art Online Auction**
www.onlineposterauction.com/

Authors

Are all the "important" writers here? Alas, no matter who is on your list of important writers, the answer must be "no." There is a site for an author only if someone has the desire and the ability to write it. Fortunately, many academics, the main sources of these pages, have both.

❏ **Sholom Aleichem**
www.sholom-aleichem.org.

❏ **Maya Angelou**
www.cwrl.utexas.edu/~mmaynard/Maya/
maya5.html

❏ **Isaac Asimov**
www.clark.net/pub/edseiler/WWW/
asimov_home_page.html

❏ **Margaret Atwood**
www.web.net/owtoad/toc.html

❏ **Jane Austen**
uts.cc.utexas.edu/~churchh/janeinfo.html

❏ **Pearl S. Buck**
Dept.english.upenn.edu/Projects/Buck/

❏ **Albert Camus**
www.sccs.swarthmore.edu/~pwillen1/lit/
indexa.htm

❏ **Raymond Carver**
world.std.com/~ptc

❏ **Willa Cather**
icg.harvard.edu/~cather/

❏ **G. K. Chesterton**
www.chesterton.org/

❏ **Arthur C. Clarke**
www.lsi.usp.br/~rbianchi/clarke

❏ **E. L. Doctorow**
www.albany.edu/tree-tops/docs.writers-inst/
doctorow.html

❏ **F. Scott Fitzgerald**
www.pbs.org/kteh/amstorytellers/bios.
html

❑ **Charles Frazier**
www.sc.edu/library/spcoll/amlit/frazier/
frazier.html

❑ **Nathaniel Hawthorne**
www.tiac.net/users/eldred/nh/hawthorne.
html

❑ **Joseph Heller**
www.levity.com/corduroy/heller.htm

❑ **Herman Hesse**
www.mcl.ucsb.edu/hesse/

❑ **Zora Neale Hurston**
pages.prodigy.com/zora/

❑ **Samuel Johnson**
www.ozemail.com.au/~reidb/index.htm

❑ **James Joyce**
www.cohums.ohio-state.edu/english/
organizations/ijjf/

❑ **Franz Kafka**
www.temple.edu/kafka/

❑ **Jack Kerouac**
www.levity.com/corduroy/kerouac.htm

❑ **Barbara Kingsolver**
www.kingsolver.com/

❑ **Jack London**
sunsite.berkeley.edu/London/

❑ **Gabriel Garcia Marquez**
www.kirjasto.sci.fi/marquez.htm

Herman Melville
www.melville.org/

❏ **John Milton**
www.mindspring.com/~verax/milton.htm

❏ **Thomas Pynchon**
pete.pomona.edu/pynchon/

❏ **Anne Rice**
www.annerice.com/

❏ **Tom Robbins**
www.rain.org/~da5e/tom_robbins.html

❏ **John Steinbeck**
www.wwu.edu/~stephan/Steinbeck/index.
html

❏ **August Strindberg**
www.extrapris.com/astrindberg.html

❏ **Amy Tan**
www.luminarium.org/contemporary/
amytan/

❏ **J. R. R. Tolkien**
www.csclub.uwaterloo.ca/u/relipper/tolkien/
rootpage.html

❏ **Mark Twain**
marktwain.miningco.com/

❏ **Jules Verne**
www.math.technion.ac.il/~rl/JulesVerne/
biblio/

❏ **Kurt Vonnegut**
www.duke.edu/~crh4/kv/kv.html

❏ **Alice Walker**
www.luminarium.org/contemporary/alicew/

❏ **Evelyn Waugh**
e2.empirenet.com/~jahvah/waugh/

❏ **Rebecca Wells**
www.ya-ya.com/

❏ **Walt Whitman**
Memory.loc.gov/ammem/wwhome.html

❏ **Tom Wolfe**
www.tomwolfe.com/

Aviation and Aerospace

There's a lot of hot stuff here, from private pilots to World War II to airline disasters.

❏ **Aerospace Resources on the Internet**
www.cranfield.ac.uk/cils/library/subjects/airmenu.htm

❏ **Air Affair**
www.airaffair.com/

❏ **Aircraft Owners and Pilots Association**
www.aopa.org/

❏ **AirNav**
www.airnav.com/

❏ **Airshow.com**
www.airshow.com/

❏ **Aviation Digest**
www.avdigest.com/default.html

❏ **Be A Pilot**
www.beapilot.com/

❑ **Canadian Snowbirds**
www.snowbirds.dnd.ca/

❑ **FAA's Web Site**
www.faa.gov/

❑ **Flights of Inspiration**
www.fi.edu/flights/

❑ **Flying Tigers**
www2.gol.com/users/sychang/WB/

❑ **Helicopter Association**
www.rotor.com/

❑ **International Council of Airshows**
www.airshows.org/

❑ **International Organization of Women Pilots**
www.ninety-nines.org/

❑ **Major Airline Disasters**
dnausers.d-n-a.net/dnetGOjg/Disasters.htm

❑ **National Aviation Hall of Fame**
www.nationalaviation.org/

❑ **National Soaring Museum**
www.soaringmuseum.org/

❑ **Photovault's Aerospace and Aviation**
www.photovault.com/Link/Technology/
AerospaceMaster.html

❑ **San Diego Aerospace Museum**
www.aerospacemuseum.org/

❑ **Scramble**
www.scramble.nl/

❑ **Spitfire Is 60**
www.deltaweb.co.uk/spitfire/index.htm

❑ **Student Pilot Network**
www.ufly.com/

❑ **The Aviation History On-Line Museum**
www.aviation-history.com/

❑ **Top 10 Airline Disasters**
www.planet101.com/airdisasters.htm

❑ **U.S. Wings Bomber Jackets**
www.pilotshops.com/

❑ **Ultralight Flying Magazine**
www.ulflyingmag.com/

❑ **U.S. Navy Blue Angels**
www.blueangels.navy.mil/

❑ **Women In Aviation Resource Center**
www.women-in-aviation.com/

Award Givers

*These sites evaluate other sites and hand out
awards in the form of small graphics that can be
displayed on winning sites. These are good
places to start the hunt for quality.*

❑ **Cool at Web**
www.web-search.com/cool.html

❑ **Cyber-Teddy**
www.cyberteddy-online.com/

❑ **High Five**
www.highfive.com/

❑ **Lycos Top 5%**
point.lycos.com/categories/

❑ **Magellan 4-Star**
www.mckinley.com

❑ **Tech Sightings**
www.techsightings.com/

❑ **Top 50 Sites That Download Quickly**
www.zazz.com/fast50/index.shtml

❑ **USA Today Hot Site**
www.usatoday.com/life/cyber/ch.htm

Best, Hot, Cool

Someone somewhere has decided that the sites on these lists are worthy of a look. They usually are.

❑ **25 Most Useful Sites**
www3.zdnet.com/yil/content/depts/useful/
25mostuse.html

❑ **All the Best Cool Sites on the Web**
www.best-cool-sites.com/

❑ **Best of the Web**
botw.org/

❑ **Canadian Cool Site of the Week**
www.escape.ca/~keir/cdncool/

❑ **Cool Central Site of the Day**
www.coolcentral.com/day/

❑ **Cool NASA Web Sites**
www.nasa.gov/cool.html

❑ **Cool Sites For Kids**
www.ala.org/alsc/children_links.html

❑ **Cool Site of the Day**
cool.infi.net/

❑ **Cool Tool of the Day**
www.cooltool.com/

❑ **Cybertown's Site of the Week**
www.cybertown.com/spider.html

❑ **Daily Web Site**
www.dailywebsite.com/

❑ **Dr. Webster's Site of the Day**
www.drwebster.com/

❑ **Dynamite Sites of the Night**
www.netzone.com/~tti/dsotn.html

❑ **Family Site of the Day**
www.worldvillage.com/famsite.htm

❑ **Internet Top Ten**
www.chartshow.co.uk/

❑ **Lynx of the Week**
web-star.com/lotw/lotw.html

❑ **Projectcool Sightings**
www.projectcool.com/sightings/

❏ **Too Cool**
www.toocool.com/

❏ **Web Today Destinations**
www.web-today.net/webtoday/

❏ **WELL-Chosen Sites**
www.well.com/pointers.html

❏ **Xplore Site of the Day**
www.explore.com/xplore500/medium/
menu.html

❏ **Z Best Sites Around**
www.zbsa.com/

Books and Reading

If you are the kind of person who must tear yourself away from a book to even look at this list, you will find further temptations here.

❏ **1st Books**
www.1stbooks.com/

❏ **A Word A Day**
www.wordsmith.org/awad/index.html

❏ **African American Literature**
Aalbc.com/

❏ **Afterhours Inspirational Stories**
inspirationalstories.com/

❏ **Banned Books On-Line**
www.cs.cmu.edu/Web/People/spok/banned-books.html

❑ **Banned Books Week**
www.ala.org/bbooks/

❑ **Bilingual Books For Kids**
www.bilingualbooks.com/

❑ **BookFinder.com**
www.bookfinder.com/

❑ **The Bookmine**
www.bookmine.com/

❑ **Books That Changed My Life**
www.well.com/user/woodman/books.html

❑ **BookWeb**
www.ambook.org

❑ **Candlelight Stories**
www.CandlelightStories.com/

❑ **Concordances of Great Books**
www.concordance.com/

❑ **Cybereditions**
Cybereditions.com/

❑ **Downloadable Books Online**
www.crystalinks.com/booksonline.html

❑ **Electronic Text Center**
etext.lib.virginia.edu/uvaonline.html

❑ **Fray**
www.fray.com/

❑ **Gemini Rare Art Books**
www.geminibooks.com/

❑ **Linda's Used Books**
www.doubledouble.net/books.htm

❑ **Luminarium**
www.luminarium.org/lumina.htm

❑ **Most Frequently Banned Books**
www.cs.cmu.edu/People/spok/most-banned.html

❑ **Online Literature Library**
www.literature.org/Works/

❑ **Printing Press as an Agent of Change**
virtual.park.uga.edu/~hypertxt/eisenstein.html

❑ **Project Gutenberg**
www.promo.net/pg/

❑ **Serious Fiction**
www.sau.edu/CWIS/Internet/Wild/Refdesk/Howgood/Bookbyte/serious.htm

Business—Finance and Investing

The financial community has discovered that many regular Internet users are also investors. Accordingly, many attractive sites promote their wares.

❑ **Armchair Millionaire**
www.armchairmillionaire.com/

❑ **Bank of America**
www.BankAmerica.com/

❑ **Bschool.com**
www.bschool.com/

❑ **Bloomberg Personal**
www.bloomberg.com/

❑ **Charles Schwab**
www.schwab.com/

❑ **Day Traders**
www.daytraders.com/

❑ **Dogs of the Dow**
www.dogsofthedow.com/

❑ **Final Bell**
www.sandbox.net/finalbell/pub-doc/home.
html

❑ **Free Stock Quotes**
www.freerealtime.com/

❑ **International Monetary Fund**
www.imf.org/

❑ **Investor Links**
www.investorlinks.com/

❑ **Message Media**
www.messagemedia.com/

❑ **Money Advisor**
www.moneyadvisor.com/

❑ **Motley Fool**
www.fool.com/

❑ **Nasdaq**
www.nasdaq.com/

❏ **New York Stock Exchange**
www.nyse.com/

❏ **Silicon Investor**
www.techstocks.com/

❏ **Standard and Poor**
www.stockinfo.standardpoor.com/

❏ **Stock Club**
stockclub.com/

❏ **Stock Smart**
www.stocksmart.com/

❏ **StockMaster**
www.stockmaster.com/

❏ **StreetEYE Index**
www.streeteye.com/

❏ **Wells Fargo**
www.wellsfargo.com/

❏ **World Bank**
www.worldbank.org/

❏ **Worldly Investor**
www.worldlyinvestor.com/

❏ **Young Investor**
www.younginvestor.com/

Business—General

This list is a potpourri of everything related, even in a vague way, to business. For pure entertainment, and even nostalgia, don't miss the 50 Best Commercials.

❏ **50 Best Commercials**
adage.com/news_and_features/
special_reports/commercials

❏ **Advertising Age**
www.adage.com/

❏ **Better Business Bureau**
www.bbbonline.org

❏ **BigBook**
www.bigbook.com/

❏ **Bschool.com**
www.bschool.com/

❏ **Business.com**
www.business.com/

❏ **Business School Site Index**
www.herts.ac.uk/business/site.htm

❏ **CardWeb**
www.ramresearch.com/

❏ **Company Sleuth**
www.companysleuth.com/

❏ **Dow Jones Business Directory**
businessdirectory.dowjones.com/

❏ **Executive PayWatch**
www.paywatch.org/

❏ **Forbes**
www.forbes.com/

❑ **Fortune 500**
cgi.pathfinder.com/fortune/fortune500/
index.html

❑ **Franchise Info**
www.frannet.com/

❑ **Harvard Business School**
www.hbs.edu/

❑ **Industry.net**
www.industry.net

❑ **Industry Week**
www.industryweek.com/

❑ **InfoUSA**
www.lookupusa.com/

❑ **ITEX Barter**
www.tradebanc.com/

❑ **NewsPage**
www.newspage.com/

❑ **Nightly Business Report**
www.nightlybusiness.org

❑ **Researching Companies on the Internet**
home.sprintmail.com/~debflanagan/

❑ **Smart Business Supersite**
www.smartbiz.com/

❑ **Tax Information For Business**
www.irs.ustreas.gov/prod/bus_info/

❑ **Wharton Business Knowledge**
knowledge.wharton.upenn.edu/

Calendars

Fun and perhaps an occasional necessity.

❏ **Algebra: Fun with Calendars**
math.rice.edu/~lanius/Lessons/calen.html

❏ **American Secular Holidays Calendar**
www.smart.net/~mmontes/ushols.html

❏ **Ancient Calendars**
physics.nist.gov/GenInt/Time/ancient.html

❏ **Calendar Zone**
www.calendarzone.com/

❏ **Chinese Calendar**
www.cnd.org/Other/calendar.html

❏ **Famous Birthdays**
www.famousbirthdays.com/

❏ **International Elections Calendar**
www.klipsan.com/calendar.htm

❏ **One-World Global Calendar**
www.zapcom.net/phoenix.arabeth/1world.
html

❏ **Phases of the Moon**
www.lunaroutreach.org/phases/phases.cgi

❏ **Virtual Perpetual Calendars**
www.vpcalendar.net/

Career/Jobs

Not all sites here will suit you, but all are worth a look. See also Resume Services.

❏ **4Work**
www.4work.com/

❏ **America's Job Bank**
www.ajb.dni.us/index.html

❏ **Ask the Headhunter**
www.asktheheadhunter.com/

❏ **Best Jobs USA**
www.bestjobsusa.com/

❏ **BrassRing.com**
www.brassring.com/

❏ **Brave New Work World**
www.newwork.com/

❏ **C++ Jobs**
www.cplusplusjobs.com/

❏ **Career Central**
www.careercentral.com/index.asp

❏ **Career City**
www.careercity.com/

❏ **Career Exposure**
www.careerexposure.com/index2.html

❏ **Career Internetworking**
www.careerkey.com/

❏ **Career Resource Center**
www.careers.org/

❏ **Career.com**
www.career.com/

❑ **CareerBuilder Network**
www.careerbuilder.com/

❑ **CareerMart.com**
www.careermart.com/

❑ **CareerMosaic**
www.careermosaic.com/

❑ **CareerPath**
careerpath.com/

❑ **CareerPro**
www.career-pro.com/index.htm

❑ **CareerWeb**
www.careerweb.com/

❑ **Computer Programming Jobs**
www.developers.net/

❑ **Computer Jobs**
www.computerjobs.com/

❑ **ComputerWork**
www.computerwork.com/

❑ **Eagleview**
www.eagleview.com/

❑ **Employease**
www.employease.com/

❑ **Entry Level Job Seeker Assistant**
Members.aol.com/Dylander/jobhome.html

❑ **Environmental Jobs and Careers**
www.ejobs.org/

❏ **First Steps in the Hunt**
www.interbiznet.com/hunt/

❏ **GetWork Network**
www.getwork.net/

❏ **HeadHunter**
www.headhunter.net/

❏ **Help-Wanted Page**
www.helpwantedpage.com/

❏ **High Technology Careers Magazine**
www.hightechcareers.com/

❏ **High-Tech Career Fairs**
www.cfcjobs.com/

❏ **HotJobs**
www.hotjobs.com/

❏ **HotJobs 2000**
www.hotjobs2000.com/

❏ **Java Jobs Online**
javajobs.com/

❏ **Job Doctor**
www.thejobdr.com/

❏ **Job Resource**
www.thejobresource.com/

❏ **Job Search Services**
www.job-searcher.com/

❏ **JobDirect**
www.jobdirect.com/

❏ **JobEngine**
www.jobengine.com/

❏ **JobHunt**
www.job-hunt.org/resume.shtml

❏ **JobOptions**
www.joboptions.com

❏ **Jobs by State**
www.coolworks.com/showme/state.htm

❏ **Jobs Online**
www.jobs-online.net/

❏ **JobSafari**
www.jobsafari.com/

❏ **Jobtrak**
www.jobtrak.com/

❏ **Job Warehouse**
www.jobwarehouse.com/

❏ **JobWeb**
www.jobweb.org/

❏ **Monster Board**
www.monster.com/

❏ **NationJob**
www.nationjob.com/

❏ **NetJobs**
www.netjobs.com:8000/

❏ **Software Jobs**
www.softwarejobs.com/

❏ **Startups.com**
www.startups.com/jobboard/

❏ **Summer Jobs**
www.summerjobs.com/

❏ **TechNet**
www.techemployment.com/

❏ **TechSearch**
www.jobsight.com/

❏ **Telecommuting Jobs**
www.tjobs.com/

❏ **Temp 24-7**
www.temp24-7.com/

❏ **The ESL Job Center**
www.pacificnet.net/~sperling/jobcenter.html

❏ **The Guide to Internet Job Searching**
www.chicagojobs.org/book.html

❏ **TV Jobs**
www.tvjobs.com/

❏ **Virtual Job Fair**
www.vjf.com/

❏ **Web Jobs USA**
www.webjobsusa.com/

Cars and Trucks

*You can get advice, check out parts, or kick the
tires of a new car. You could even buy one.*

❏ **American Automobile Association**
www.aaa.com/

❏ **Ames Cars**
www.amescars.com

❏ **Autobytel.com**
www.autobytel.com/

❏ **Auto Mall USA**
www.automallusa.com/

❏ **Auto Web**
www.autoweb.com

❏ **AutoConnect**
www.autoconnect.net/

❏ **Automobile Leasing**
www.mindspring.com/~ahearn/lease/lease.
html

❏ **Autopedia**
www.autopedia.com/

❏ **Autorama**
autorama.com/

❏ **Autorow**
www.autorow.com/

❏ **AutoSite**
www.autosite.com/

❏ **Car Center**
www.intellichoice.com/

❏ **Car Connection**
www.thecarconnection.com/

❏ **Car Place**
www.thecarplace.com/

❏ **CarPoint**
Carpoint.msn.com/

❏ **Car Recalls**
www.nhtsa.dot.gov/cars/problems/

❏ **CarsDirect.com**
www.carsdirect.com/

❏ **Car Tracker**
www.cartrackers.com/

❏ **Cartalk**
www.cartalk.com/

❏ **Classic Cars**
www.classicar.com/museums/aacalbry/
aacalbry.htm

❏ **Crash Tests**
www.crashtest.com/intro/index.htm

❏ **IntelliChoice Car Center**
www.carpoint.msn.com/

❏ **Kelley Blue Book**
www.kbb.com/index.html

❏ **Land Rover**
www.landrover.com/

❏ **Motor Trend**
www.motortrend.com/

❏ **NASCAR Online**
www.nascar.com/

❏ **NHTSA: National Highway Traffic Safety Administration**
www.nhtsa.dot.gov/

❑ **Popular Mechanics**
popularmechanics.com/

❑ **Special Cars**
www.specialcar.com/

❑ **Virtual Auto Parts Store**
gate.cruzio.com/~vaps/

❑ **Weekend Mechanics Club**
www.weekendmechanicsclub.com

Cities

Many of these U.S. city sites emphasize the official arm of the government; others focus on tourism.

❑ **Albuquerque**
www.albuquerque.com/

❑ **Anaheim**
Anaheim.areaguides.net/

❑ **Annapolis**
www.capitalonline.com/tour/

❑ **Anchorage**
www.alaska.net/~acvb

❑ **Arlington**
www.ci.arlington.tx.us/

❑ **Atlanta**
www.atlanta.org/

❑ **Atlantic City**
www.virtualac.com/

❏ **Aurora**
aurora.areaguides.net/

❏ **Austin**
austin.citysearch.com/

❏ **Baltimore**
baltimore.areaguides.net/

❏ **Birmingham**
birmingham.areaguides.net/

❏ **Boise**
www.ci.boise.id.us/

❏ **Boston**
www.ci.boston.ma.us/

❏ **Buffalo**
buffalo.areaguides.net/

❏ **Charlotte**
charlotte.areaguides.net/

❏ **Chicago**
www.centerstage.net/chicago/

❏ **Cincinnnati**
www.cincinnati.com

❏ **Cleveland**
www.cleveland.com/

❏ **Colorado Springs**
www.csurf.com/csurf/tour.html

❏ **Columbus**
www.ci.columbus.oh.us/

❏ **Corpus Christi**
corpuschristi.areaguides.net/

❏ **Dallas**
www.ci.dallas.tx.us/

❏ **Denver**
www.denver.org/

❏ **Detroit**
www.ci.detroit.mi.us/

❏ **El Paso**
elpaso.areaguides.net/

❏ **Fairbanks**
www.areaguide.net/fairbanks

❏ **Fort Worth**
www.fortworth.acn.net/

❏ **Fresno**
www.ci.fresno.ca.us/

❏ **Gainesville**
www.state.fl.us/gvl/

❏ **Hartford**
www.hartford.com/

❏ **Honolulu**
www.co.honolulu.hi.us/

❏ **Houston**
www.ci.houston.tx.us

❏ **Indianapolis**
www.indplsconnect.com/

❏ **Jacksonville**
www.ci.jax.fl.us/

❏ **Kansas City**
www.kcmo.org/

❏ **Las Vegas**
www.lasvegas.org/

❏ **Lexington**
lexington.areaguides.net/

❏ **Little Rock**
www.littlerock.com/

❏ **Long Beach**
www.ci.long-beach.ca.us/

❏ **Los Angeles**
www.ci.la.ca.us/

❏ **Louisville**
www.louisville-visitors.com/

❏ **Memphis**
www.ci.memphis.tn.us/

❏ **Mesa**
www.ci.mesa.az.us/

❏ **Miami**
www.miami.com/

❏ **Milwaukee**
www.ci.mil.wi.us/

❏ **Minneapolis**
www.citypages.com/

❏ **Nashville**
Nashville.citysearch.com/

❏ **New Orleans**
www.noconnect.com/

❏ **Newark**
newark.areaguides.net/

❑ **Oakland**
oakland.areaguides.net/

❑ **Oklahoma City**
oklahomacity.areaguides.net/

❑ **Omaha**
www.ci.omaha.ne.us/

❑ **Philadelphia**
www.gophila.com/

❑ **Phoenix**
www.ci.phoenix.az.us/

❑ **Pittsburgh**
www.pittsburgh.net/

❑ **Portland**
www.ci.portland.or.us/

❑ **Raleigh**
www.raleigh-nc.org/

❑ **Reno**
www.reno.com/

❑ **Riverside**
www.ci.riverside.ca.us/

❑ **Sacramento**
sacramento.areaguides.net/

❑ **Salt Lake City**
www.ci.slc.ut.us/

❑ **San Antonio**
www.sachamber.com/Tourism.htm

❑ **San Diego**
www.seesandiego.com/

❑ **San Francisco**
sanfrancisco.citysearch.com/

❑ **San Jose**
www.sanjose.org/nsapi/sj_home_page

❑ **Santa Fe**
www.santafe.org/

❑ **Santa Monica**
pen.ci.santa-monica.ca.us/

❑ **Savannah**
www.savannah-online.com/

❑ **Seattle**
www.pan.ci.seattle.wa.us/

❑ **Shreveport**
www.ci.shreveport.la.us/

❑ **St. Louis**
stlouis.areaguides.net/

❑ **St. Paul**
stpaul.areaguides.net/

❑ **Syracuse**
www.syracuse.com/

❑ **Tallahassee**
www.tallahassee.com/

❑ **Tampa**
tampa.areaguides.net/

❏ **Toledo**
www.ci.toledo.oh.us/Homepage.html

❏ **Tucson**
www.ci.tucson.az.us/

❏ **Tulsa**
www.ci.tulsa.ok.us/

❏ **Virginia Beach**
virginiabeach.areaguides.net/

❏ **Washington, D.C.**
www.washington.org/

❏ **Wichita**
www.wichita.com.

College

Most college sites represent a specific school. You can find yours by using a search engine. The generic sites are listed here.

❏ **Adults Back to College**
www.back2college.com/

❏ **All About College**
www.allaboutcollege.com/

❏ **All Campus In-Sites**
www.allcampus.com/

❏ **American Universities**
www.planet-hawaii.com/global/universy.html

❏ **Business Schools**
ulinks.com/list/business.html

❏ **Campus Tours**
www.campustours.com/

❏ **College Admission and Scholarship Counseling**
www.college-scholarships.com/ssac.htm

❏ **College Choice Website**
www.gseis.ucla.edu/mm/cc/home.html

❏ **College Edge**
www.collegeedge.com/

❏ **Community College Web**
www.mcli.dist.maricopa.edu/cc/

❏ **CyberCampus**
www.cybercampus.com/

❏ **Dormitories Around the World**
www.heim1.tu-clausthal.de/
studentenwohnheime/english/

❏ **FinAid!**
www.finaid.org/

❏ **Gradschools.com**
www.gradschools.com/

❏ **Main Quad**
www.mainquad.com/

❏ **Peterson's Education Supersite**
www.petersons.com/

❏ **Security on Campus**
Campussafety.org/

❏ **Study Abroad**
www.nrcsa.com/

❑ **Study Abroad Directory**
www.studyabroad.com./

❑ **United States Student Association**
www.essential.org/ussa/ussa.html

❑ **Western Governors University**
www.wgu.edu/wgu/index.html

Computer History

Several people give us details, sometimes from their personal experiences, about how it all started. See also Internet History.

❑ **Charles Babbage Institute**
www.cbi.umn.edu/

❑ **Computer Chronicles: From Stone to Silicon**
despina.advanced.org/22522/

❑ **Computer Museum**
www.tcm.org/

❑ **Digital Moments**
www.menuez.com/

❑ **First Virtual Mousepad Museum**
www.expa.hvu.nl/ajvdhek/

❑ **History of Computing**
ei.cs.vt.edu/~history/index.html

❑ **History of Shareware**
www.pslweb.com/history.htm

❑ **History of the Apple Computer**
www.apple-history.com/

❏ **IEEE Annals of the History of Computing**
www.computer.org/annals/

❏ **Macintosh Museum**
www.macintoshos.com/macintosh.museum/
index.shtml

❏ **Memoir: Homebrew Computer Club**
www.bambi.net/bob/homebrew.html

❏ **Mind machine Museum**
userwww.sfsu.edu/~hl/mmm.html

❏ **MouseSite**
sloan.stanford.edu/MouseSite/

❏ **Obsolete Computer Museum**
www.ncsc.dni.us/fun/user/tcc/cmuseum/
cmuseum.htm

❏ **Silicon Valley History and Future**
www.internetvalley.com/introduction.html

❏ **Smithsonian Computer History**
www.si.edu/resource/tours/comphist/
computerl.htm

❏ **Software History Center**
www.softwarehistory.cor/

❏ **Tech Museum of Innovation**
www.thetech.org/

❏ **The Machine That Changed the World**
ei.cs.vt.edu/~history/TMTCTW.html

❏ **The Revolutionaries**
www.thetech.org/revolutionaries/

❏ **Univac Memories**
www.fourmilab.ch/documents/univac/
index.html

Computer Organizations
and Events

If you want to join or go to a convention, or just figure out who these people are, check out their sites.

❏ **ACM Association of Computing Machinery**
info.acm.org

❏ **Association of Internet Professionals**
www.association.org

❏ **AWC Association for Women in Computing**
www.awc-hq.org/

❏ **Comdex**
www.comdex.com/comdex/owa/home

❏ **ICCA Independent Computer Consultants Association**
www.icca.org/

❏ **ICCP Institute for Certification of Computing Professionals**
www.iccp.org/

❏ **IEEE Institute of Electrical and Electronics Engineers**
www.computer.org/

❏ **TechCalendar**
www.techweb.com/calendar/

Computer Science

Sites of interest to computer science people,
especially those related to the Internet, are
spread throughout this book. This list merely
mentions a few topics more specific to the field.

❏ **Advanced Computing Laboratory**
www.acl.lanl.gov/

❏ **Center for Information Technology**
logic.stanford.edu/cit/

❏ **Computing Dictionary**
www.InstantWeb.com/foldoc/

❏ **Diccionario—Terminos Informaticos**
www.ctv.es/USERS/angelaj/

❏ **Computing Languages List**
union.ncsa.uiuc.edu/HyperNews/get/
computing/lang-list.html

❏ **Glossary of Computer Abbreviations**
www.access.digex.net/~ikind/babel.html

❏ **IEEE Standards**
standards.ieee.org/

❏ **Internet Parallel Computing Archive**
www.hensa.ac.uk/parallel/

❏ **LinuxWorld**
www.linuxworld.com/

❑ **Microsoft Research**
www.research.microsoft.com/

❑ **MIT Media Lab**
www.media.mit.edu/

❑ **National Center for Supercomputing Applications**
www.ncsa.uiuc.edu/

❑ **Online Computing Journals**
www.utexas.edu/computer/vcl/journals.html

❑ **Soft Center**
www.softcenter.se/

❑ **Sony Computer Science Lab**
www.csl.sony.co.jp/Unified Computer
Science TR Index Unified

❑ **Technology Transfer Virtual Library**
www.nttc.edu/gov/other/tech.html

❑ **U.S. Computer Science Departments**
www.utexas.edu/computer/vcl/acadcomp.
html

❑ **Unix Guru Universe**
www.ugu.com/

❑ **World Lecture Hall**
www.utexas.edu/world/lecture/cs/

Computers—Programming and Languages

A small collection of sites. See also *Java and Home Page—HTML Help Sites.*

❑ **Ask the SQL Pro**
www.inquiry.com/techtips/thesqlpro/

❑ **C++ Report**
www.creport.com/

❑ **Carl and Gary's Visual Basic Home Page**
www.cgvb.com/

❑ **CGI Resource Index**
www.cgi-resources.com/

❑ **Computer Programming Languages**
src.doc.ic.ac.uk/bySubject/Computing/
Languages.html

❑ **From the Ground Up: A Guide to C++**
library.advanced.org/3074/

❑ **Game Design 101**
www.gamecenter.com/Features/Exclusives/
Design/

❑ **Game Programming Megasite**
www.perplexed.com/GPMega/

❑ **IBM COBOL**
www.software.ibm.com/ad/cobol/

❑ **Introduction to C Programming**
devcentral.iftech.com/learning/tutorials/

❑ **Object Oriented Software**
www.soft-design.com/softinfo/sdc.html

❑ **Open Source Software**
public.resource.org/

❑ **Qbasic**
www.qbasic.com/

Cool Companies

Know them by their cool sites. Several of them have multimedia features.

❏ **American Express**
www6.americanexpress.com/travel/index.
html

❏ **Ben and Jerry's Ice Cream**
www.benjerry.com/

❏ **Boeing**
www.boeing.com/

❏ **Bristol-Myers Squibb**
www.bristolmyers.com/

❏ **Campbell Soup**
www.campbellsoup.com/

❏ **Caterpillar**
www.caterpillar.com/

❏ **Charles Schwab**
www.schwab.com/

❏ **Clark Bar**
www.clarkbar.com/

❏ **Colgate-Palmolive**
www.colgate.com

❏ **ConAgra**
www.conagra.com/

❏ **Crayola**
www.crayola.com/crayola/

❏ **Disney**
www.disney.com/

❏ **Dunlop Tires**
www.dunloptire.com/

❏ **Dupont**
www.dupont.com/

❏ **E*Trade**
www.etrade.com/

❏ **Eastman Kodak**
www.kodak.com/

❏ **Eli Lilly**
www.elililly.com/

❏ **Esprit**
www.esprit.com/

❏ **F.A.O. Schwarz**
www.faoschwarz.com/

❏ **FedEx**
www.fedex.com/

❏ **Ferrari**
www.ferrari.it/ferrari/

❏ **Fila**
www.fila.com/

❏ **Ford**
www2.ford.com/

❏ **GTE**
www.gte.com/

❏ **Gatorade**
www.gatorade.com/

❏ **General Electric**
www.ge.com/

❑ **Gillette**
www.gillette.com/

❑ **HBO**
www.hbo.com/

❑ **Hershey**
www.hersheys.com/

❑ **Home Depot**
www.homedepot.com/

❑ **Honda**
www.honda.com/

❑ **Iams**
www.iams.com/

❑ **J.P. Morgan**
www.jpmorgan.com/

❑ **Johnson & Johnson**
www.johnsonjohnson.com/

❑ **Kellogg's**
www.kelloggs.com/

❑ **Kmart**
www.kmart.com/

❑ **Kraft**
www.kraftfoods.com/

❑ **Levi Strauss Jeans**
www.levi.com/

❑ **McDonald's**
www.mcdonalds.com/

❑ **MCI Worldcom**
www.mciworldcom.com/

❏ **Merck**
www.merck.com/

❏ **Mobil**
www.mobil.com/

❏ **Nestle**
www.nestle.com/

❏ **Nordstrom**
www.nordstrom.com/

❏ **Office Depot**
www.officedepot.com/

❏ **OfficeMax**
www.officemax.com/

❏ **Pepsi**
www.pepsiworld.com/index2.html

❏ **Pfizer**
www.pfizer.com/

❏ **Polaroid**
www.polaroid.com/

❏ **Saatchi and Saatchi**
www.saatchi-saatchi.com/

❏ **Sears**
www.sears.com/

❏ **Sharp Electronics**
www.sharp-usa.com/

❏ **Starbucks**
www.starbucks.com

❏ **Taco Time**
www.tacotime.com/

❏ **Tide ClothesLine**
www.clothesline.com/

❏ **UPS**
www.ups.com

❏ **Volkswagen**
www3.vw.com/

❏ **Xerox**
www.xerox.com/

Consumer Information

If you never knew there were so many things to worry about, you will after you peruse some of these sites.

❏ **AMA Health Information**
www.ama-assn.org/consumer.htm

❏ **Anti-Telemarketer Source**
www.izzy.net:80/~vnestico/t-market.html

❏ **Appliance**
www.appliance.com/

❏ **AttorneyLocate.com**
www.attorneylocate.com

❏ **Choosing a Mover**
www.amconf.org/

❏ **Consumer Drug Info**
www.fda.gov/cder/consumerinfo/default.htm

❏ **Consumer Handbook**
www.pueblo.gsa.gov/crh/respref.htm

❏ **Consumer Information Center**
www.pueblo.gsa.gov/

❏ **Consumer Law**
consumerlawpage.com:80/

❏ **Consumer Product Safety Commission**
www.cpsc.gov:80/

❏ **Consumer Protection**
www.wmbakerassociates.com/consprotect.
html

❏ **Consumer World**
www.consumerworld.org/

❏ **Federal Trade Commission Home Page**
www.ftc.gov/

❏ **Food Safety**
www.foodsafety.org/

❏ **Home Inspection FAQs**
www.creia.com/faq.htm

❏ **How to Choose a Builder**
www.buildithomeplans.com/chsebuild.htm

❏ **Insurance Company Ratings**
www.insure.com/ratings/index.html

❏ **Pyramid Schemes and Chain Letters**
dcn.davis.ca.us/~btcarrol/skeptic/pyramid.
html

❏ **Retail Sales Ploys**
www.bookouts.com/snake.htm

❑ **Scambusters**
www2.scambusters.com/scambusters/

❑ **Smart Consumer**
www.worth.com/articles/PC0.html

❑ **Stop the Junk Mail**
www.stopjunk.com/

❑ **Street Cents**
www.halifax.cbc.ca/streetcents/

Counting

We do a lot of counting on the Internet. And, for some reason, the favorite number is 100.

❑ **The 100 Best Comics of the Century**
www.smartworld.com/comics/comics.html

❑ **100 Best Companies to Work For**
www.randomhouse.com/modernlibrary/
100best/

❑ **100 Black Men Of America, Inc.**
www.100blackmenofcharlotte.org/

❑ **100 High-Tech Career Fairs**
www.network-events.com/

❑ **100 Hot Web Sites**
www.100hot.com/

❑ **100 Largest Foreign Investments in the U.S.**
www.ofii.org/

❑ **100 Largest U.S. Banks**
www.moneypage.com/pulse/cont100.htm

❏ **100% Jokes**
www.100percentjokes.com/

❏ **100 Most Handsome Indian Men**
www.indiatimes.com/100handsomemen/

❏ **100 Recettes Bistro**
photo.net/wtr/100-things.html

❏ **100 Things**
www.acorn-online.com/100thing.htm

❏ **100 Things To Make Your Web Site Better**
photo.net/wtr/100-things.html

❏ **100 Years of Radio**
www.alpcom.it/hamradio/

❏ **Top 100 Newspapers**
www.interest.com/top100.html

❏ **Billboard Hot 100**
www.billboard.com/charts/hot100.asp

❏ **Daily 100**
www.80s.com/Entertainment/Movies/

❏ **Dogomania**
www.dogomania.com/topsites/

❏ **Fantasy Baseball**
www.letsplay2.com/baseball/top100.cfm

❏ **Life Online: Millennium**
www.lifemag.com/Life/millennium/events/
100.html

❏ **Occult 100**
www.occult100.com/topsites.cgi?lavender

❑ **Stories of the Century**
www.newseum.org/century/

❑ **The Shopping 100**
www.shopping100.com/

❑ **Time 100: Artists and Entertainers**
cgi.pathfinder.com/time/time100/index.html

❑ **Top 100 Brain Structures**
www.med.harvard.edu/AANLIB/cases/
caseM/case.html

❑ **Top 100 Computer Magazines**
www.internetvalley.com/top100mag.html

❑ **Top 100 Hospitals**
www2.hcia.com/100top/98/

❑ **Top 100 Posters**
www.allwall.com/asp/Top100-asp/_/
NV--1_F1/1.asp

❑ **Top 100 Screen Savers**
www.top100screensavers.com/

❑ **Veronica Top 100 Countdown**
www.veronica.nl/top100/

❑ **Web 100**
www.web100.com/

❑ **Web Shopping 100**
www.shopping100.com

❑ **Wisecat's Top 100**
wisecat.co.uk/

❑ **World's 100 Most Endangered Sites**
www.worldmonuments.org/list.html

❏ **Worldwide Genealogy Topsites**
www.worldwide-top100.net/tops5/

Cycling

*Touring, racing, or just out for an afternoon spin?
It's all here on the Internet.*

❏ **Aardvark Cycles**
www.aardvarkcycles.com/

❏ **Aegis Handmade Carbon Fiber Bicycles**
www.aegisbicycles.com/

❏ **Bicycles on the Web**
www.cis.upenn.edu/~vinson/cycling.html

❏ **Bicycling's Skill Center**
www.bicyclingmagazine.com/skill/

❏ **Bike Club Directory**
www.adventuresports.com/asap/bike/
bikeclub.htm

❏ **Bike Current**
web2.thesphere.com/bikecurrent/

❏ **Bike Ride Online**
www.bikeride.com/

❏ **BikeSite**
Bikesite.com/

❏ **Chain Reaction Bicycles**
www.chainreactionbicycles.com/

❏ **Club Tread Reports**
www.bltg.com/ctreport/default.html

❑ **Ellsworth Handcrafted Bicycles**
ellsworthbicycles.com/

❑ **Gary Fisher Mountain Bikes**
www.fisherbikes.com/

❑ **Hanebrink Bicycles and Forks**
www.hanebrinkforks.com/

❑ **Jaanus Bicycles**
www.jaanusbicycles.com/

❑ **Klein Bicycles**
www.kleinbikes.com/

❑ **Le Tour de France**
www.letour.fr/

❑ **Mountain Biking**
xenon.stanford.edu/~rsf/mtn-bike.html

❑ **National Bicycle Greenway**
www.bikeroute.com/

❑ **Project New Zealand**
www.projectnz.org/

❑ **Science of Cycling**
www.exploratorium.edu/cycling

❑ **Specialized**
www.specialized.com/

❑ **Stolen Bike Registry**
www.nashville.net/cycling/stolen.html

❑ **Tailwinds**
www.voyager.net/tailwinds/

❏ **Trek Bikes**
www.trekbikes.com/

❏ **Unicycling**
ecstasy.winternet.com/usa/

❏ **USA Cycling Online**
www.usacycling.org/

❏ **U.S. Deaf Cycling Homepage**
home.earthlink.net/~skedsmo/usdca.htm

❏ **VeloNews**
www.greatoutdoors.com/velonews/

❏ **Velo Pages**
www.access.ch/velopages/

❏ **WWW Bicycle Lane**
www.cs.purdue.edu/homes/dole/bike.html

Don'tcha Just Love It?

There is nothing that we can add to a description of these sites that their titles don't already tell.

❏ **Antsite**
www.gizmonics.com/

❏ **Band-Aids**
www.savetz.com/bandaid/

❏ **Carousels**
www.carousel.org/

❏ **Carrot Top**
www.carrottop.com/

❏ **Casbah**
www.dsiegel.com/

❑ **Cyrano Love Letters**
www.nando.net/toys/cyrano.html

❑ **Famous Last Words**
web.mit.edu/randy/www/words.html

❑ **Fractal Cow Studio**
www.fractalcow.com/

❑ **Joe Boxer**
www.joeboxer.com/

❑ **The Box**
www.sixsides.com/

Economics

If you are an economist, an economist-in-training, or just a bystander who wonders how the economy runs, it's all here for the taking.

❑ **Brookings: Economic Studies**
www.brook.edu/ES/ES_HP.HTM

❑ **Bureau of Economic Analysis**
www.bea.doc.gov/

❑ **Bureau of National Affairs**
www.bna.com/

❑ **Cato Institute**
www.cato.org/

❑ **Dismal Scientist**
www.dismal.com/

❑ **Econometrics Laboratory**
elsa.berkeley.edu/eml/

❏ **Economic Analysis**
www.bea.doc.gov/

❏ **Economic Research Service**
www.econ.ag.gov/

❏ **Economic Statistics Briefing**
www.whitehouse.gov/fsbr/esbr.html

❏ **Economic Time Series**
www.economagic.com/

❏ **Economics Working Paper Archive**
econwpa.wustl.edu/

❏ **Federal Budget**
www.whitehouse.gov/OMB/budget/index.
html

❏ **Federal Government Spending**
www.fedmoney.com/fedspending2.html

❏ **FinWeb**
www.finweb.com/

❏ **Foundation for Teaching Economics**
www.fte.org/

❏ **History of Economics**
home.tvd.be/cr27486/hope.html

❏ **IMF World Economic Outlook**
www.imf.org/external/pubs/ft/weo/1999/
01/index.htm

❏ **Inflation Calculator**
www.westegg.com/inflation/

❏ **Institute for International Economics**
www.iie.com/

❏ **Internet Resources for Economists**
econwpa.wustl.edu/EconFAQ/EconFAQ.html

❏ **Journal of Labor Economics**
www.journals.uchicago.edu/JOLE/home.html

❏ **National Bureau of Economic Research**
nber.harvard.edu/

❏ **One Line Economics**
aris.ss.uci.edu/econ/personnel/kawa/aphorism.html

❏ **RAND Journal of Economics**
www.rand.org/misc/rje

❏ **Study Tips for Economics Courses**
www.utexas.edu/student/lsc/handouts/1409.html

❏ **The Economist**
www.economist.com/

❏ **The Journal of Law & Economics**
www.journals.uchicago.edu/JLE/home.html

Electronic Commerce

Lots of help is available to both fledgling and established e-commerce merchants, as well as their customers.

❏ **3 Steps to E-Commerce Success**
www.e-commerce1.com/

❏ **BizBot: Online Business Directory**
www.bizbot.org/

❑ **Clue to Internet Commerce**
www.ppn.org/clue

❑ **CommerceNet**
www.commerce.net/

❑ **CyberCash**
www.cybercash.com/

❑ **Cybersmarts**
www.ftc.gov/bcp/conline/pubs/online/
cybrsmrt.htm

❑ **E-Commerce Advisory Council**
www.e-commerce.ca.gov/

❑ **E-Commerce News**
www.internetnews.com/ec-news/

❑ **E-Commerce Times**
www.ecommercetimes.com/

❑ **E-Commerce Treasure Trove**
www.wilsonweb.com/commerce/

❑ **E-Commerce Exchange**
www.eccx.com/

❑ **E-Commerce Guide**
ecommerce.internet.com/

❑ **E-Commerce Resources**
www.acumen-solutions.co.uk/ecommerce/
resource.htm

❑ **Federal E-Commerce Program**
ec.fed.gov/

❑ **ICAT Commerce Online**
www.icat.com/

❏ **Internet Tax Freedom Act**
www.house.gov/chriscox/nettax/

❏ **Jumbostore**
www.jumbostore.com/

❏ **Public Eye**
www.thepubliceye.com/

❏ **StoreFront**
www.storefront99.com/

❏ **The Usenet Marketplace FAQ**
www.fmn.net/FAQ/

❏ **TRUSTe Directory**
www.truste.com/

❏ **Upside Online**
www.upside.com/

❏ **Web Marketing Today**
www.wilsonweb.com/wmt/

Education

Educators were early users of the Internet, and their contributions continue to be significant. There is a rich trove of education materials on the Internet for current and future educators.

❏ **21st Century Teachers Network**
www.21ct.org/

❏ **Association for the Advancement of Computing in Education**
curry.edschool.Virginia.edu/aace/

❏ **Center for Media Literacy**
www.medialit.org/

❏ **Choices Education Project**
www.brown.edu/Research/Choices/

❏ **Cisco Educational Archive**
sunsite.unc.edu/cisco/cisco-home.html

❏ **Education Week**
www.edweek.org/

❏ **Education Online**
www.strategicstudies.com/eduOnline_pgr.html

❏ **Education Resources Information Center (ERIC)**
ericir.sunsite.syr.edu/

❏ **Educational Software Institute**
www.edsoft.com/

❏ **InfoList for Teachers**
www.electriciti.com/

❏ **International WWW Schools Registry**
web66.coled.umn.edu/schools.html

❏ **James Randi Educational Foundation**
www.randi.org/

❏ **K-12+ Schools Web Site Index**
www.tenet.edu/education/main.html

❏ **KinderArt**
www.kinderart.com/

❏ **Learner Online**
www.learner.org/

❏ **Multimedia Classrooms**
www.tcimet.net/mmclass/index.htm

❏ **Natural Discovery Cave**
discovery.thorntons.co.uk/

❏ **On Line Funding Resources**
k12science.ati.stevens-tech.edu/
connect/funding.html

❏ **PBS TeacherSource**
www.pbs.org/teachersource/

❏ **Scholastic Place**
www.scholastic.com/

❏ **School Enrollment**
www.census.gov/population/www/socdemo/
school.html

❏ **School.Net**
k12.school.net/

❏ **Schoolhouse Videos**
www.schoolroom.com/

❏ **SyllabusWeb**
www.syllabus.com/

❏ **Teacher Source**
www.pbs.org/teachersource/

❏ **Teachers Helping Teachers**
www.pacificnet.net/~mandel/

❏ **Teachers On-line**
www.smuhsd.k12.ca.us/Resources/
tresources/Teachers_On-line/
teachers_on-line.html

❑ **Teaching with Historic Places**
www.cr.nps..gov/nr/twhp/home.html

❑ **Teachnet**
www.teachnet.com/

❑ **Young Adult Reading**
www.docker.com/~whiteheadm/yaread.html

❑ **The Educational Testing Service Network**
www.ets.org/

❑ **ThinkQuest**
www.thinkquest.org/

❑ **U.S. Department of Education**
www.ed.gov/

❑ **Xpeditions**
www.nationalgeographic.com/resources/ngo/
education/xpeditions/

Entertainment

*The entertainment category is a big winner on
the Internet, attracting everything from simple
games to conglomerates.*

❑ **Ain't It Cool News**
www.aint-it-cool-news.com/

❑ **Arts and Entertainment**
www0.delphi.com/arts/

❑ **As the Web Turns**
www.metzger.com/soap/cast.html

❑ **Cirque de Soleil**
www.cirquedusoleil.com/

❑ **International Clown Hall of Fame**
www.clownmuseum.org/chofhist.html

❑ **Costume Source**
www.milieux.com/costume/source.html

❑ **Disney**
www.disney.com/

❑ **Click-and-Drag Poetry**
prominence.com/java/poetry/

❑ **Elvis Lives**
wsrv.clas.virginia.edu/~acs5d/elvis.html

❑ **Entertainment Charts**
www.worldcharts.nl/

❑ **Faces**
www.corynet.com/faces/

❑ **Fireworks Central**
www.pcpros.net/~runrath/fireworks.html

❑ **Juggling**
www.juggling.org/

❑ **Klutz**
www.klutz.com/

❑ **Mr. Showbiz**
www.mrshowbiz.com/

❑ **Mungo Park**
www.mungopark.com

❑ **Second City**
www.secondcity.com/

❑ **Soundbites**
www.soundbites.com/

❑ **The Station**
www.station.sony.com

❑ **Ticketmaster**
www.ticketmaster.com

❑ **Wizard of Oz**
www.thewizardofoz.com/

Entrepreneurs

The Internet is a natural for entrepreneurs who are starting on a shoestring. There are many experienced folks who offer help along the way.

❑ **20 Reasons**
www.net101.com/reasons.html

❑ **Books and Software for the Entrepreneur**
www.business-plan.com/

❑ **Business Know-How**
www.businessknowhow.com/

❑ **Business Resource Center**
www.morebusiness.com/

❑ **Entrepreneur America**
www.entrepreneur-america.org/

❑ **Entrepreneur Book Store**
www.joem.com

❑ **Entrepreneur Magazine**
www.entrepreneurmag.com/magentre/
business_bytes.html

❏ **Entrepreneurial Parent**
www.en-parent.com/

❏ **Entrepreneurs Anonymous**
www.clickit.com/booksinprogress/
arthurlipper/ea.htm

❏ **Entrepreneurs and Business Leaders**
www.spartacus.schoolnet.co.uk/business.htm

❏ **Entrepreneurs' Foundation**
www.the-ef.org/

❏ **Entrepreneurs' Help Page**
www.tannedfeet.com/

❏ **Entre-World**
www.entreworld.org

❏ **Great Idea Finder**
www.businessknowhow.com/

❏ **Idea Cafe**
www.ideacafe.com/

❏ **Minority Business Entrepreneur**
www.mbemag.com/

❏ **MoneyHunter**
www.moneyhunter.com/

❏ **Score**
www.score.org/

❏ **Social Entrepreneurs**
www.centerforrenewal.org/from_the_front___/
Social_Entrepreneurs/social_entrepreneurs.
html

❏ **The Center to Develop Women Entrepreneurs**
www.cob.sjsu.edu/dept/cdwe/CDWE.html

❏ **WWW Entrepreneurial Business Directory**
worldentre.com/bizdir.htm

❏ **Young Entrepreneurs' Organization**
www.yeo.org/

Family

There are many resources on the Internet for families. See also Consumer Information and Kid Stuff.

❏ **ABC's of Parenting**
www.abcparenting.com/

❏ **Ask Great-Granny**
http://www.crm.mb.ca/granny/granny.html#toc

❏ **BABYNAMES.COM**
www.babynames.com/

❏ **Babynet**
www.babynet.com/

❏ **Baby Place**
www.baby-place.com/

❏ **Babyonline**
www.babyonline.com/

❏ **Baby-Proof Home**
www.babyproof.com/

❏ **BabyUniverse.com**
www.babyuniverse.com/index.asp?adopt

❏ **Bilingual Parenting**
www.byu.edu/~bilingua/

❏ **BlackFamilies**
www.blackfamilies.com/

❏ **College Savings Plans**
www.collegesavings.org/

❏ **Cybermom**
www.thecybermom.com/

❏ **Family Education Network**
www.families.com/

❏ **Family Internet**
www.familyinternet.com/

❏ **Family Workshop**
www.ctw.org/

❏ **Family.com**
www.family.go.com/

❏ **Foster Parent Community**
www.fosterparents.com/

❏ **Guide to Toys and Play**
www.kidsource.com/kidsource/content/
toys_ply.html

❏ **Homearts**
www.homearts.com/

❏ **Keeping Kids Reading**
www.tiac.net/users/maryl/

❏ **Moms Online**
ww103w.momsonline.com/

❏ **Nap Time Notes**
www.ddc.com/napnotes/

❏ **National Center for Fathering**
www.fathers.com/

❏ **Parent Soup**
www.parentsoup.com/

❏ **ParenthoodWeb**
www.parenthoodweb.com/

❏ **Parenting Q & A**
www.parenting-qa.com/

❏ **ParentsPlace**
www.parentsplace.com/

❏ **Raisin**
www.raisinnet.com/

❏ **Single and Custodial Father's Page**
www.single-fathers.org/

❏ **Stork Net**
pages.prodigy.com/gifts/stork.htm

❏ **Summer Camps**
www.camppage.com/

❏ **The National Parenting Center**
www.tnpc.com/

❏ **WholeFamily Center**
www.wholefamily.com/

Festivals

These days, "festival" usually means "film festival." But we were able to find a few of the traditional kind.

❏ **American Dance Festival**
www.americandancefestival.org/home.html

❏ **Edinburgh Fringe Festival**
www.edfringe.com/

❏ **Festival Finder**
www.festivalfinder.com/

❏ **Festivals.com**
festivals.com/

❏ **Film Festivals.com**
www.filmfestivals.com/

❏ **Juggling Festivals**
www.juggling.org/festivals/

❏ **Lilith Fair**
www.lilithfair.com/

❏ **National Asparagus Festival**
www.oceana.net/naf/

❏ **New England Folk Festival**
www.ultranet.com/~neffa

❏ **New Orleans Jazz and Heritage Festival**
www.nojazzfest.com/

❏ **North Carolina Literary Festival**
sunsite.unc.edu/litfest/

❏ **Oregon Shakespeare Festival**
www.orshakes.org/

❑ **Prescott Park Arts Festival**
www.artfest.org/

❑ **What's Going On**
www.whatsgoingon.com/

Financial Aid

Here it is, most—if not all—the information available, all in one place.

❑ **CollegeNET**
www.collegenet.com/

❑ **Collegiate Funding Group**
www.collegiatefunding.com/

❑ **eStudentLoan**
www.estudentloan.com/

❑ **fastWEB**
www.fastweb.com/fastweb/

❑ **FinAid**
www.finaid.org/

❑ **Financial Aid from U.S. Dept. of Education**
www.ed.gov/prog_info/SFA/StudentGuide/

❑ **Financial Aid Resource Center**
www.theoldschool.org/

❑ **Free Application for Federal Student Aid (FAFSA)**
www.fafsa.ed.gov/

❑ **GoCollege**
www.gocollege.com

❏ **Paying for College**
www.theoldschool.org

❏ **Private Funding Information**
www.rams.com/

❏ **Resource Pathways**
www.collegeaid.com/

❏ **Sallie Mae's Financial Aid 101**
www.salliemae.com/aud/faa

❏ **Scholarship Resource Network**
www.rams.com/srn/

❏ **Scholarship Search**
www.collegeboard.org/fundfinder/html/
ssrchtop.html

❏ **Stafford Loans**
www.ed.gov/prog_info/SFA/StudentGuide/
1998-9/loan.html

❏ **United Negro College Fund**
www.uncf.org/

Fitness and Health

If you are "into" fitness, you can find several useful sites on this list. If you have avoided the prospect, you still might find some inspiration here.

❏ **2nd Opinion**
www.2ndopinionstore.com/main.htm

❏ **Achoo**
www.achoo.com

❏ **American Medical Association**
www.ama-assn.org/

❏ **Arthritis Foundation**
www.arthiritis.org/

❏ **Ask the Dietician**
www.dietitian.com/

❏ **Black Stump Medical Page**
werple.net.au/~lions/medical.htm

❏ **Cool Medical Site of the Week**
www.hooked.net/users/wcd/cmsotw.html

❏ **Cool Running**
www.coolrunning.com/

❏ **CyberDiet**
www.cyberdiet.com/

❏ **Family Internet**
www.familyinternet.com

❏ **Fast Food Facts**
www.olen.com/food/

❏ **Fitness Online**
www.fitnessonline.com/

❏ **Fitness Zone**
www.fitnesszone.com/

❏ **Food Allergy Network**
www.foodallergy.org/

❏ **Friends' Health Connection**
www.48friend.com/

❏ **Go Ask Alice**
www.alice.columbia.edu/

❏ **Go Get Fit**
www.lifetimetv.com/WoSport/gogetfit/

❏ **Health Action Network Society**
www.hans.org/

❏ **Health and Wellness Center**
shn.webmd.com/index.html

❏ **Health Information Database**
chid.nih.gov/

❏ **Health Mall**
www.hlthmall.com/

❏ **Health-Center**
www.healthguide.com/

❏ **Healthfinder**
www.healthfinder.gov

❏ **HealthTouch**
www.healthtouch.com/

❏ **HealthWorld Online**
www.healthy.net/

❏ **Heart Preview Gallery**
sln2.fi.edu/biosci/preview/heartpreview.html

❏ **Heat Waves**
www.redcross.org/disaster/safety/heat.html

❏ **HouseCall**
www.HouseCall.com/

❏ **Learn CPR**
www.learncpr.org/index.html

❏ **Life Matters**
lifematters.com/

❏ **Light Living**
www.lightliving.com/

❏ **MD Interacative**
www.mit.edu/afs/athena/user/p/a/pandre/
www/

❏ **Medical Breakthroughs**
www.ivanhoe.com/

❏ **Medicine Box**
www.medicinebox.com/

❏ **Merck Manual**
www.merck.com/

❏ **National Physique Committee**
www.getbig.com/info/npc.htm

❏ **Power Bar**
www.powerbar.com/

❏ **QuackWatch**
www.quackwatch.com/

❏ **RxTV**
www.rxtv.com/

❏ **Safe Within**
www.safewithin.com/

❏ **SleepNet**
www.sleepnet.com

❏ **Thrive**
www.thriveonline.com/

❏ **Video Fitness**
videofitness.com/

❏ **Wellness Web**
www.wellweb.com/

❑ **What Does It Take to Be Healthy?**
5aday.nci.nih.gov/

❑ **Women's Health**
www.4women.gov/

❑ **World Health Organization**
www.who.ch/Welcome.html

❑ **World Wellness on the Web**
wellness.uwsp.edu/

Food

Good but not necessarily good for you.

❑ **Bagel Oasis**
www.bageloasis.com/

❑ **Bread Recipe**
www.breadrecipe.com/

❑ **Cakes**
www.cakerecipe.com/

❑ **Chef Talk**
www.cheftalk.com/

❑ **CompuCook**
www.compucook.com/

❑ **Cookie Recipes**
www.cookierecipe.com/

❑ **Cooking Messy**
www.messygourmet.com/

❑ **Culinaria**
www.culinaria.com

Food

❏ **Diabetic Gourmet Magazine**
diabeticgourmet.com/

❏ **Digital Cookie**
www2.digitalcookie.com/cookie/

❏ **Edible Insects**
www.eatbug.com/

❏ **Epicurious**
www.epicurious.com/

❏ **EthelM Chocolates**
www.ethelm.com

❏ **Fast Food Facts**
www.olen.com/food/

❏ **Food and Drug Administration**
www.fda.gov/

❏ **Food Network**
www.foodtv.com

❏ **French Fries**
www.tx7.com/fries/

❏ **Godiva Chocolates**
www.godiva.com/

❏ **Gourmet Connection Network**
gourmetconnection.com/

❏ **Gourmet Mushrooms and Mushroom Products**
www.gmushrooms.com/

❏ **Gourmet World**
www.gourmetworld.com/

❏ **Grits**
grits.com

❏ **Gumbo Pages**
www.gumbopages.com/

❏ **Inquisitive cook**
www.inquisitivecook.com/

❏ **International Food Information Council**
ificinfo.health.org/

❏ **Internet Chef**
www.ichef.com

❏ **Jell-o**
www.jell-o.com/jell-o100/

❏ **Kitchen Link**
www.kitchenlink.com/

❏ **Kosher Grocer**
www.koshergrocer.com/

❏ **M & Ms Network**
www.m-ms.com/

❏ **Meals for You**
www.mymenus.com/

❏ **Meals**
www.meals.com

❏ **Nantucket Nectars**
www.juiceguys.com/index.htm

❏ **Planet Ketchup**
www.ketchup.wonderland.org/

❑ **Popcorn Institute**
www.popcorn.org/mpindex.htm

❑ **Ragu Presents**
www.eat.com/

❑ **Recipe Dude**
recipedude.com/

❑ **RiceWeb**
www.riceweb.org/

❑ **SmellTheCoffee**
www.smellthecoffee.com/

❑ **Soup Recipes**
www.souprecipe.com/

❑ **Star Chefs**
www.starchefs.com/

❑ **Sushi Guide**
nmd.hyperisland.se/studentzone/crew2/
martin_ragnevad/

❑ **Tastykake**
www.tastykake.com/

❑ **Top Secret Recipes**
www.topsecretrecipes.com/

❑ **Vegetarian Epicure**
www.vegetarianepicure.com/

Free Stuff

*Entire books have been written about free stuff
on the Internet. We were picky about what we
selected.*

❏ **3D Cafe's Free Stuff**
www.3dcafe.com/asp/freestuff.asp

❏ **Absolutely Free Screen Savers**
www.free-search.com/

❏ **Bienvenue sur Free**
www.free.fr/

❏ **Free Internet Encyclopedia**
clever.net/cam/encyclopedia.html

❏ **Free'n Cool**
free-n-cool.com/

❏ **Free Center**
www.freecinter.com/

❏ **Free Site**
www.thefreesite.com/

❏ **Free Stuff Central**
www.freestuffcentral.com/

❏ **Free Stuff Sites**
www.thingamabob.com/

❏ **Free Stuff**
www.tectonicdesigns.com/contest/
cindex.cgi?view=k

❏ **Jelly Belly**
www.jellybelly.com/

❏ **Post-It Notes**
www.mmm.com/psnotes

❏ **TheFreeSite.com**
www.thefreesite.com/

❏ **Tool-Free Free Stuff**
pages.prodigy.com/ULDE89A/

❏ **Volition Free Stuff Center**
www.volition.com/free.html

Games and Puzzles

Some of these are multimedia sites.

❏ **A Collection of Word Oddities and Trivia**
members.aol.com/gulfhigh2/words.html

❏ **Adenaline Vault**
www.avault.com/

❏ **Backgammon on the Web**
www.statslab.cam.ac.uk/~sret1/
backgammon/main.html

❏ **BaliHighway**
www.balihighway.com/

❏ **Bethesda Softworks**
www.bethsoft.com/

❏ **Big Top**
www.bigtop.com/

❏ **Bingo Zone**
www.bingozone.com/

❏ **Brain Teasers and Puzzles**
www.brainbashers.com/

❏ **Buzzword Bingo**
www.buzzwordbingo.com/

❏ **Card Trick Central**
web.superb.net/cardtric

❏ **Checkers**
www.cs.caltech.edu/~vhuang/cs20/c/applet/

❏ **Chess on the Net**
www.chessed.com/

❏ **Classic Board Games**
www.gamestorm.com/puzzleandboard/
classicboard/

❏ **Connect Four**
www.gamegate.com/connect4.

❏ **Cryptographs**
www.cryptograph.com/

❏ **Dockingbay**
www.scd.uu.se;~johnn/

❏ **DomainGames**
www.domaingames.com/

❏ **Droodles**
www.webonly.com/droodles/index.html

❏ **Electric Origami**
www.ibm.com/Stretch/EOS/

❏ **Free Puzzle Collections**
www.freepuzzles.com/

❏ **Game Briefs**
www.gamebriefs.com/index.htm

❏ **Game Guides**
www.gameguides.com/index.html

❏ **Game-Land**
www.game-land.com/

❏ **Games.com**
www.games.com/

❑ **Games Domain**
www.gamesdomain.co.uk/

❑ **Gamesmania**
www.gamesmania.com/

❑ **GameSpy**
www.gamespy.com/

❑ **GT Interactive**
www.gtinteractive.com/

❑ **Happy Puppy**
www.happypuppy.com

❑ **Jeopardy**
www.station.sony.com/jeopardy/

❑ **Kid Crosswords and Other Puzzles**
www.kidcrosswords.com/

❑ **Monopoly**
www.monopoly.com/

❑ **Mr. Edible Starchy Tuber Head**
winnie.acsu.buffalo.edu/potatoe/index.html

❑ **Paintball Net**
www.paintball-net.com/

❑ **Parcheesi**
www.rhodes.com/parcheesi/

❑ **Phonetic**
www.phonetic.com

❑ **Pooh Sticks**
pooh.muscat.co.uk/pooh-sticks/

❑ **Puzzle Depot**
www.puzzledepot.com/

❏ **PuzzlesCom Home**
www.puzzles.com/

❏ **Revenge of the Cow-Boy**
www.sega.com/multimedia/games/cow/

❏ **Riddle du Jour**
www.dujour.com/riddle/

❏ **Riddler**
www.riddler.com

❏ **Scrabble**
www.scrabble.com/

❏ **Sharky Games**
www.sharkygames.com/

❏ **Stomped!**
www.stomped.com/

❏ **Terra: Battle for the Outland**
www.kaon.com/

❏ **The Official Microsoft Games Web Site**
www.microsoft.com/games/

❏ **The Trivia Portal**
www.funtrivia.com/

❏ **Tiddlywinks**
www.tiddlywinks.org/

❏ **Tic Tac Toe**
scv.bu.edu/Games/tictactoe

❏ **Trivial Pursuit**
www.trivialpursuit.com/

❏ **Uproar**
www.uproar.com

❏ **Wheel of Fortune**
www.station.sony.com/wheel/

❏ **Word Zap**
www.wordzap.com/

Gardening

*What's your pleasure? Terrariums? Giant
pumpkins? Window boxes? Check it out.*

❏ **Biological Control**
www.nysaes.cornell.edu/ent/biocontrol/

❏ **Bloom**
homearts.com/depts/garden/00gardc1.htm

❏ **Butterfly Gardens**
www.uky.edu/Agriculture/Entomology/
entfacts/misc/ef006.htm

❏ **Cherry Blossom Gardens**
www.garden-gifts.com/

❏ **Daylilies**
www.daylilies.com/daylilies/

❏ **Design Your Own Sprinkler System**
www.netyard.com/jsa/spklr.htm

❏ **Dig**
www.digmagazine.com/

❏ **Don't Panic Eat Organic**
www.rain.org/~sals/my.html

❏ **Garden Escape**
www.garden.com/

❏ **Garden.com**
www.garden.com/

❏ **Gardening in the South**
www.geocities.com/RainForest/Vines/8060

❏ **Gardening Supplies and Equipment**
www.the-garden-gnome.com/products/
shops_01.shtml

❏ **GardenWeb**
www.gardenweb.com/

❏ **Giant Pumpkins**
www.athenet.net/~dang/pumpkins.html

❏ **Growing Vegetables at Home**
www.hoptechno.com/book26.ht.

❏ **Heirloom Seeds**
www.heirloomseeds.com/

❏ **Houseplant Care**
www.hoptechno.com/book26.htm

❏ **Internet Shrine to the Tomato**
members.aol.com/rbi82/randy/tomato.
html#grow

❏ **Interurban Water Farms**
www.interurban.com/

❏ **Kootensaw Dovecotes**
www.dovecotes.co.uk/

❏ **Landscaping to Attract Birds**
www.fws.gov/r9mbmo/pamphlet/attract.html

❏ **Life in a Terrarium**
homearts.com/depts/garden/botanica/
01botab4.htm

❏ **Master Composter**
www.mastercomposter.com/

❏ **Natural Pest Control Center**
www.invisiblegardener.com/

❏ **Organic Gardening**
www.organicgardening.com/

❏ **Perennial Gardening**
www.natures-domain.com/perennials.htm

❏ **Perennial Gardening in Containers**
www.nwseed.com/nursery/perennial_
gardening_in_container.htm

❏ **Proper Pruning**
aggie-horticulture.tamu.edu/extension/
pruning/pruning.html

❏ **Rhododendron and Azaleas**
www.users.fast.net/~shenning/rhody.html

❏ **Seeds of Change**
www.seedsofchange.com/

❏ **Seeds Unique**
www.seedsonline.com/

❏ **The Savage Garden**
www.thesavagegarden.com/

❏ **Traditional Gardening**
www.traditionalgardening.com/

❑ **Understanding Your Soil**
homepages.which.net/~fred.moor/soil/
formed/f01.htm

❑ **Urban Garden**
www.urbangarden.com/

❑ **US Soil, Inc.**
www.planters2.com/

❑ **Vegetable Gardening**
www.backyardgardener.com/veg/

❑ **Vegetable Gardening FAQ Page**
faq.gardenweb.com/faq/cornucop/

❑ **Virtual Garden**
www.vg.com/

❑ **Weed Identification**
ext.agn.uiuc.edu/wssa/subpages/weed/
herbarium0.html

❑ **Yard-Care Answer Guy**
www.yardcare.com/

Genealogy

As a hobby, genealogy used to mean a lot of leg-work and letter writing. Now the Internet makes it so easy that genealogy has become a main-stream activity.

❑ **A to Z of Irish Genealogy**
www.irish-insight.com/a2z-genealogy/

❑ **Ancestry**
www.ancestry.com/

❑ **Barrel of Genealogy Links**
cpcug.org/user/jlacombe/mark.html

❑ **Cool Sites for Genealogists**
www.cogensoc.org/cgs/cgs-cool.htm

❑ **Cyndi's List of Genealogical Sites**
www.cyndislist.com/

❑ **Everton's Genealogical Helper**
www.everton.com/

❑ **FamilyHistory.com**
www.familyhistory.com/

❑ **Family Tree Maker Software**
www.familytreemaker.com

❑ **Folks Online**
www.folksonline.com/bbs3/

❑ **Genealogy.com**
www.genealogy.com/

❑ **Genealogy Abbreviations**
home.sprynet.com/~lgk71/2abbrevi.htm

❑ **Genealogy Gateway**
www.polaris.net/~legend/listings/listings.html

❑ **Genealogy Home Page**
www.genhomepage.com/

❑ **Genealogy Is My Hobby**
home.earthlink.net/~middleton/

❑ **Genealogy Online**
www.genealogy.org/

❑ **Genealogy Software**
www.toltbbs.com/~kbasile/software.html

❑ **Genealogy Today**
www.genealogytoday.com/

❑ **Genealogy Toolbox**
genealogy.tbox.com/

❑ **Genealogy Unlimited**
www.itsnet.com/home/genun/public_html/

❑ **Genealogy Web Search Tools**
www.gensource.com/

❑ **International Black Sheep Society**
homepages.rootsweb.com/~blksheep/
index.html

❑ **Italian Genealogy**
www.daddezio.com/

❑ **Janyce's Root Diggin' Dept.**
www.janyce.com/gene/rootdig.html

❑ **Journal of Online Genealogy**
www.onlinegenealogy.com/

❑ **LDS Genealogy Records**
www.onlinegenealogy.com/

❑ **Mayflower Web Page**
members.aol.com/calebj/mayflower.html

❑ **Nova's Genealogy Page**
www.buffnet.net/~nova/

❑ **Searchable Genealogy Links**
www.bc1.com/users/sgl/

❑ **Surname Finder**
searches.rootsweb.com/

❑ **The Genealogy Register**
www.genealogyregister.com/

Government

The government was one of the earliest and biggest users of computers. It continued the pattern by being one of the earliest and biggest users of the Internet. Just about every government office and agency has a Web presence, and it is often easier to find information there than to contact an official—a real person—by telephone. We list only a few sites here; many others can be found under more specific titles.

❏ **Congressional Information**
clerkweb.house.gov/

❏ **Draft Registration Online**
www.sss.gov/

❏ **FBI – Most Wanted**
www.fbi.gov/mostwant/topten/tenlist.htm

❏ **FBI Records Search**
www.policeguide.com/cgi-bin/criminal-search

❏ **Internal Revenue Service**
www.irs.ustreas.gov

❏ **Library of Congress**
www.loc.gov/

❏ **Meet the Mayors**
www.mayors.org/

❏ **National Security Study Group**
www.nssg.gov/

❏ **Patent Web Databases**
www.uspto.gov/

❏ **Social Security Online**
www.ssa.gov/SSA_Home.html

❏ **Terrorist Group Profiles**
web.nps.navy.mil/~library/tgp/tgpmain.htm

❏ **U.S. Census Bureau**
www.census.gov/

❏ **U.S. Patent and Trademark Office**
www.uspto.gov

❏ **U.S. Postal Service**
www.usps.gov/

❏ **U.S. Bill of Rights**
constitution.by.net/BillOfRights.html

❏ **U.S. Government Printing Office**
www.access.gpo.gov/index.html

❏ **U.S. Senate**
www.senate.gov

❏ **United States Government Manual**
www.access.gpo.gov/nara/browse-gm.html

❏ **White House**
www.whitehouse.gov/

Graphics—Animation

Those specifically interested in animation will find sites of interest in this list, but will probably be even more interested in the multimedia lists.

❏ **3D Animated Flags**
www.3dflags.com/

❑ **3D Café**
www.3dcafe.com/

❑ **3D PixRay**
www.fortunecity.com/victorian/summit/180/

❑ **3Dize**
www.3dize.com/

❑ **A Touch of This**
www.atouchofthis.com/

❑ **Absolutely Free Animation**
www.altwebmasters.com/aag/

❑ **Alex's Animated Gif Shop**
www.wsdaents.com'

❑ **Animated Banners**
www.mugs-n-more.com/main.htm

❑ **Animate Gif Artist Guild**
www.agag.com/

❑ **Animated Gifs**
www.angelfire.com/tx/willowrose/
animate.html

❑ **Animation**
www.ogle.com/

❑ **Animation 101**
library.thinkquest.org/25398/

❑ **Animation and Graphics for Your Web Site**
www.bellsnwhistles.com/

❑ **Animation Express**
www.hotwired.com/animation/

❏ **Animation Library**
www.animationlibrary.com/

❏ **Animation Magazine**
www.animag.com/

❏ **Animation World Network**
www.awn.com/

❏ **BoxTop Software**
www.boxtopsoft.com/

❏ **Clip Flicks**
www.zurqui.com/crinfocus/clip/flicks.html

❏ **Computer Animation**
www.bergen.org/AAST/ComputerAnimation/

❏ **Computer Graphics Lab**
ligsg2.epfl.ch/

❏ **Digital Character Animation**
www.rubberbug.com/

❏ **Engineering Animation**
www.eai.com/index.html

❏ **Facial Animation**
mambo.ucsc.edu/psl/fan.html

❏ **ForDyn Engineering Animation**
www.fordyn.com/

❏ **Free Clipart**
www.eclipsed.com/

❏ **Gallery of Animations**
members.tripod.com/adm/popup/roadmap.
shtml

❑ **GFDL Visualization Guide Animation**
www.gfdl.gov/~jps/GFDL_VG_Animation.html

❑ **GifWorld**
www.gifworld.com/

❑ **Gremlin Animation**
www.thegremlin.com/

❑ **HotWired Animation**
www.hotwired.com/animation/

❑ **KliK Animation**
www.klikanimation.com/

❑ **LightWork Design**
www.lightwork.com/

❑ **Lotman's Animation Art Collection**
www.lotmansart.com/

❑ **Lucasfilm**
www.lucasfilm.com/

❑ **Millanimations**
www.millan.net/anims/giffar.html

❑ **Misery Graphics**
www.itprojects.net/~den/

❑ **S/R Lab Animation**
www.srlabs.com/

❑ **UCLA Animation Workshop**
animation.filmtv.ucla.edu/

❑ **Women in Animation**
women.in.animation.org/

Graphics—Fractals

Fractal art is formed by using the computer to repeat geometric shapes with color, size, and angle variations.

❏ **Aros Fractals**
www.arosmagic.com/Fractals/default.htm

❏ **Crazy Fractals**
ourworld.compuserve.com/homepages/
pete_and_glyn/

❏ **Fantastic Fractals**
library.advanced.org/12740/cgi-bin/login.cgi

❏ **Fractal Desktop**
fractaldesktop.virtualave.net/

❏ **Fractal Domains**
www.fractaldomains.com/

❏ **Fractal Images**
www.softsource.com/fractal.html

❏ **Fractal Images**
www.maui.com/~twright/fractals/
fractals.html

❏ **Fractal Microscope**
www.ncsa.uiuc.edu/Edu/Fractal/
Fractal_Home.html

❏ **Fractal Pictures and Animations**
www.cnam.fr/fractals.html

❏ **Fractal World**
www.kcsd.k12.pa.us/~projects/fractal/

❑ **Fractals As Art**
www.cs.swarthmore.edu/~binde/fractals/

❑ **Fractals Lesson**
math.rice.edu/~lanius/frac/

❑ **MathsNet Fractals**
www.mathsnet.net/fractals.html

❑ **Sekino's Fractal Gallery**
www.willamette.edu/~sekino/fractal/
fractalhtm

❑ **sci.fractals FAQ**
www.landfield.com/faqs/sci/fractals-faq/

❑ **Sprott's Fractal Gallery**
sprott.physics.wisc.edu/fractals.htm

❑ **The Fractory**
tqd.advanced.org/3288/

Graphics—Free Stuff for Your Home Page

Many sites have made their icons and images freely available. You can copy what you want for use on your own home page.

❑ **...connected**
www.connected-media.com/

❑ **Absolutely Free Icon Library**
www.free-search.com/afil/

❑ **Angelfire**
www.angelfire.com/

❏ **Angel's Web Graphics**
www.angelswebgraphics.com/

❏ **Background Color Switcher**
www.urban75.com/Mag/java3.html

❏ **Background Graphics Archive**
www.nan.shh.fi/NAN/Shared/Backgrounds/

❏ **Background Graphics Library**
homer.coconet.com/graphlib/bckgrd1.htm

❏ **Background Sampler**
www.netscape.com/assist/net_sites/bg/
backgrounds.html

❏ **Banner Generator**
www.coder.com/creations/banner/

❏ **Barry's Clip Art**
www.barrysclipart.com/

❏ **Buttons, Bullets, and Backgrounds**
www.rewnet.com/bbb/

❏ **Cartoon Animals**
www.toontakes.com/WebArt.html

❏ **Clip Art Connection**
www.clipartconnection.com/

❏ **Clip Art Searcher**
www.webplaces.com/search/

❏ **Clip Art Universe**
www.nzwwa.com/mirror/clipart/

❏ **Clipart Castle**
www.clipartcastle.com/

❏ **Clipart.com**
www.clipart.com/

❏ **CoolGraphics.com**
www.coolgraphics.com/

❏ **CoolText**
www.cooltext.com/

❏ **Elated Web Toolbox**
www.elated.com/toolbox/

❏ **Fractal Graphics Background**
www.fractalgraphics.com.au/corp_profile/
background/

❏ **Flaming Text.com**
www.flamingtext.com/

❏ **Free Clip Art**
www.allfreeclipart.com/

❏ **Free Graphics**
www.freegraphics.com/

❏ **Free Graphics Library**
www.graphicslibrary.com/

❏ **Free Image Repository**
www.planetnetwork.com/exp4/index.htm

❏ **Graphics Depot**
www.graphicsdepot.com/

❏ **Iconographics Design**
www.iconographics.com/clip_f.htm

❏ **Image O Rama**
members.aol.com/dcreelma/imagesite/
image.htm

❏ **Images and Icons**
www.stars.com/Vlib/Authoring/Images_and_Icons.html

❏ **Inki's ClipArt**
www.inki.com/clipart/

❏ **Internet Bumper Stickers**
www.directtodave.com/ibs/

❏ **Julianne's Background Textures**
www.sfsu.edu/~jtolson/textures/textures.htm

❏ **Jumbles Animal Gallery**
www.jumblesanimalgallery.com/

❏ **Logo Design**
www.coolgraphic.som/

❏ **Pambytes Free Web Graphics**
www.pambytes.com/

❏ **Pardon My Icons**
www.zeldman.com/icon.html

❏ **Pattern Land**
www.netcreations.com/patternland/

❏ **ProDraw Graphics**
www.prodraw.net/

❏ **Rad Graphics**
www.rad-gfx.com/

❏ **Silk Purse Graphics**
mars.ark.com/~rhamstra/backgrnd.html

❏ **Texture Land**
www.meat.com/textures/

❑ **Texture Station**
www.nepthys.com/textures/

Graphics—General

Graphics are one of the major bonuses of computing. Pictures are a vast improvement over plain text.

❑ **3d Graphics Programming**
www.gamedev.net/hosted/3dgraphics/

❑ **3m Image Graphics**
www.mmm.com/imagegraphics/

❑ **ACM SIGGRAPH**
www.siggraph.org/home.html

❑ **Bozlo Beaver**
www.bozlo.com/

❑ **Cool Demos**
www-graphics.stanford.edu/demos/

❑ **Corbis**
www.corbis.com/

❑ **Design Graphics Online**
www.designgraphics.com.au/

❑ **Emm Graphics**
www.emmgraphics.com/

❑ **EyeWire**
www.imageclub.com/

❑ **Flying Circle Graphics**
www2.eos.net/speed/

❑ **Free Graphics for Your Web Page**
mem.tcon.net/users/5010/6293/index.htm

❑ **Good Earth Graphics**
www.goodearthgraphics.com/

❑ **Grafica Obscura**
www.sgi.com/grafica/

❑ **Graphic Artists Guild**
www.gag.org/

❑ **Graphic Linx**
www.graphiclinx.com/

❑ **Hey You! Graphics**
hey-you.com/collective/

❑ **Internet Ray Tracing Competition**
www.irtc.org

❑ **Lightscape**
www.lightscape.com/

❑ **Marc Yankus**
www.users.interport.net/~niceboy/portfolio/

❑ **Mastering 3D Graphics**
www.mastering3dgraphics.com/

❑ **Matrox Group**
www.matrox.com/

❑ **Pamorama**
www.pamorama.com/

❑ **Phong**
www.phong.com/

❑ **Pinsharp 3D Graphics**
www.pinsharp.demon.co.uk/

❑ **Pixel Foundary**
www.pixelfoundry.com/

❑ **Pixel Graphics Inc.**
www.pixelgraphics.on.ca/

❑ **Pixelplace**
www.pixelplace.com/

❑ **Precision Digital Images**
www.precisionimages.com/

❑ **Raytracing FAQs**
www.povray.org/documents/rayfaq/
rayfaq.html

❑ **Real 3D**
www.real3d.com/

❑ **Realm Graphics**
www.ender-design.com/rg/

❑ **Satellite Images**
www.bom.gov.au/weather/national/satellite/

❑ **Stanford Computer Graphics**
www-graphics.stanford.edu

❑ **The Graphics Gallery**
members.aol.com/Yschneller/graphics/

❑ **TheISpot**
www.theispot.com/

❑ **Themed Graphics**
members.aol.com/TikiMike/

❏ **Transparent Background Images**
members.aol.com/htmlguru/transparent_
images.html

❏ **Vision Quest**
www.boondock.com/visionquest/

❏ **Volumeone**
www.volumeone.com

Graphics—Screen Savers

*Most, but not all, of these screen savers can be
downloaded free.*

❏ **100-screen-savers.com**
www.100-screen-savers.com/

❏ **Ansel Adams Screensavers**
www.digitalwow.com/screenlogic/ansel.htm

❏ **ArtScreens**
www.artscreens.com/

❏ **Cities Screensaver**
www.design2graphics.com/html/ssaver/
ssaver_cities.html

❏ **Great Smokey Mountains Screensaver**
www.greatsmokymtns.com/

❏ **Holographic Screen Saver**
www.virtual-creations.com/

❏ **Kaleidoscope**
www.syntrillium.com/kaleidoscope/index.html

❏ **Lilli's Free Screen Savers**
www.lilli.clara.net/freesaver/

❏ **Make Your Own Screen Saver**
www.customsavers.com/

❏ **Newman's Top 10 Screen Savers**
www.top10lists.com/

❏ **Psychedelic Screen Saver**
www.synthesoft.com/psych/psych.htm

❏ **Screen Saver Heaven**
www.galttech.com/ssheaven.shtml

❏ **Screen Savers & Wall Papers**
www.usagreetings.com/screens/

❏ **Screen Savers Bonanza**
www.bonanzas.com/ssavers/

❏ **ScreenSaver**
www.screensaver.com/

❏ **Screentheme**
www.screenthemes.com/

Graphics—Software

Some are expensive professional products, some are shareware. Several have galleries.

❏ **Adobe Photoshop Web Reference**
www.adscape.com/eyedesign/photoshop/

❏ **Adobe**
www.adobe.com/

❏ **Autocad Shareware Clearinghouse**
www.cadalog.com/

❏ **Bryce Tips and Tricks**
www.kagi.com/busse/BSolutions/
Bsolutions.html

❏ **Bryce Tutorials**
www.ruku.com/bryce.html

❏ **CorelDraw**
www.corel.com/

❏ **Imagine Graphics**
www.imageinegraphics.org/

❏ **Lightwave 3D**
www.newtek.com/

❏ **Marlin Studios Graphics Machine**
www.stmuc.com/moray/

❏ **Moray Home Page**
www.stmuc.com/moray/

❏ **Paint Shop Pro Tips**
psptips.com/

❏ **Photoshop Tips**
www.mccannas.com/pshop/photosh0.htm

❏ **POV-Ray**
www.povray.org/

❏ **Rhino**
www.rhino3d.com/

❏ **Terrain Maker**
www.ericjorgensen.com/html/tm.htm

History

Both organizations and academic institutions have made use of the Internet to tell the story of the world, one chunk at a time.

❏ **1939 World's Fair**
xroads.virginia.edu/~1930s/DISPLAY/39wf/
front.htm

❏ **1968: The Whole World Was Watching**
www.stg.brown.edu/projects/1968/

❏ **Abridged History of the United States**
www.us-history.com/

❏ **Academy of Achievement**
www.achievement.org/autodoc/pagegen/
mainmenu.html?hb=1

❏ **American Civil War**
funnelweb.utcc.utk.edu/~hoemann/
cwarhp.html

❏ **American Memory**
rs6.loc.gov

❏ **American Museum of Natural History**
www.amnh.org/

❏ **American West**
www.AmericanWest.com/

❏ **Battle of Hastings 1066**
battle1066.com/

❏ **Benjamin Franklin**
sln.fi.edu/franklin/rotten.html

❏ **Black History Tour**
library.advanced.org/10320/Tourmenu.htm

❏ **British Monarchy**
www.royal.gov.uk/

❑ **Civil War: An Illinois Soldier**
www.ioweb.com/civilwar/

❑ **Child Labor in America**
www.historyplace.com/unitedstates/
childlabor/index.html

❑ **Colonial Williamsburg**
www.history.org/

❑ **Ellis Island**
www.ellisisland.org/

❑ **French and Indian War**
web.syr.edu/~laroux/

❑ **Great Chicago Fire**
www.chicagohs.org/fire/

❑ **Guts and Glory**
www.pbs.org/wgbh/pages/amex/guts/

❑ **Harappa**
www.harappa.com/

❑ **Harlem Renaissance**
harlem.eb.com/

❑ **Historical U.S. Census Data**
fisher.lib.virginia.edu/census/

❑ **History Buff**
www.historybuff.com/

❑ **History Net**
www.thehistorynet.com/

❑ **History of Money**
www.ex.ac.uk/~Rdavies/arian/llyfr.html

❑ **Horus' History Links**
www.ucr.edu/h-gig/horuslinks.html

❑ **Journey on the Underground Railroad**
www.smithsonianmag.si.edu/smithsonian/
issues96/oct96/undergroundrr.html

❑ **Kennedy Tapes**
www.cs.umb.edu/jfklibrary/tapes_1998.html

❑ **Lewis and Clark**
www.pbs.org/lewisandclark/

❑ **Martin Luther King Papers**
www.stanford.edu/group/King/

❑ **Monticello**
www.monticello.org/

❑ **Organization of American Historians**
www.indiana.edu/~oah/

❑ **Panama Canal**
www.discovery.com/stories/history/
panama/panama.html

❑ **Pop History Now**
www.bestpractices.org/

❑ **Rulers**
www.geocities.com/Athens/1058/rulers.html

❑ **Seven Wonders**
pharos.bu.edu/Egypt/Wonders/

❑ **Somme Battle 1916**
www.btinternet.com/~sommetours/

❑ **The Black History Museum**
www.afroam.org/history/history.html

❏ **The History of Computing**
ei.cs.vt.edu/~history/

❏ **The History of Mathematics**
www.maths.tcd.ie/pub/HistMath/

❏ **This Day in History**
www.historychannel.com/today/

❏ **Today in History**
memory.loc.gov/ammem/today/

❏ **U-boat Net**
uboat.net/

❏ **Vietnam Veterans Memorial Wall**
www.cpeq.com/~wall/

❏ **Women in American History**
women.eb.com/

❏ **World History Document Archives**
www.hartford-hwp.com/archives/

Hobbies and Interests

*Have we mentioned your hobby in this list?
Possibly not. We tried to present a representative
sample. See also Gardening, Cycling, Outdoor
Recreation, and Sports.*

❏ **AeroWeb**
aeroweb.brooklyn.cuny.edu/

❏ **American Kiteflyers Association**
www.aka.kite.org/

❏ **Antique Radios**
members.aol.com/djadamson/arp.html

❏ **AquaLink**
www.aqualink.com/

❏ **Autograph Central**
www.autographcentral.com

❏ **Beekeeping**
ourworld.compuserve.com/homepages/
Beekeeping/

❏ **Card Collector Link**
www.collector-link.com/cards/

❏ **Center for Puppetry Arts**
www.puppet.org/

❏ **Chinook Checkers**
www.cs.ualberta.ca/~chinook/

❏ **Classic Typewriters**
xavier.xu.edu/~polt/typewriters.html

❏ **Coin Universe**
www.coin-universe.com/

❏ **Collecting Comics**
www.collecting-comics.com/

❏ **Collecting Cuff Links**
www.cufflink.com/

❏ **CraftNet Village**
www.craftnet.org/

❏ **Crafts Galore**
www.massachusetts.net/nozzle/crafts/

❏ **Disneyananet**
www.disneyananet.com/

❑ **Estes Rockets**
www.estesrockets.com/

❑ **Gold Prospecting**
www.klws.xom/gold/gold.html

❑ **Historical Bottle Collectors**
www.av.qnet.com/~glassman/

❑ **Hobby Stores on the Net**
www.hobbystores.com/

❑ **HobbyWorld**
www.hobbyworld.com/

❑ **International Paperweight Society**
www.armory.com/~larry/ips.html

❑ **Internet Antique Shop**
www.tias.com/

❑ **Juggling**
www.juggling.org/

❑ **Knots on the Web**
www.earlham.edu/~peters/knotlink.htm

❑ **License Plates of the World**
danshiki.oit.gatech.edu/~iadt3mk/index.html

❑ **Magic Theater**
magictheater.com/index.html

❑ **MagicTricks**
www.magictricks.com/

❑ **Oragami Flowers**
www.the-village.com/origami/gallery.html

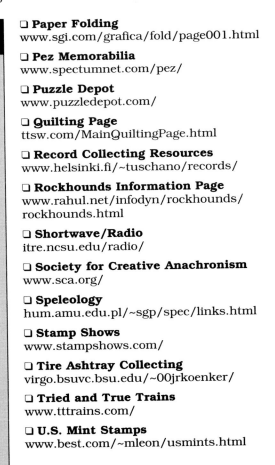

❏ **Paper Folding**
www.sgi.com/grafica/fold/page001.html

❏ **Pez Memorabilia**
www.spectumnet.com/pez/

❏ **Puzzle Depot**
www.puzzledepot.com/

❏ **Quilting Page**
ttsw.com/MainQuiltingPage.html

❏ **Record Collecting Resources**
www.helsinki.fi/~tuschano/records/

❏ **Rockhounds Information Page**
www.rahul.net/infodyn/rockhounds/
rockhounds.html

❏ **Shortwave/Radio**
itre.ncsu.edu/radio/

❏ **Society for Creative Anachronism**
www.sca.org/

❏ **Speleology**
hum.amu.edu.pl/~sgp/spec/links.html

❏ **Stamp Shows**
www.stampshows.com/

❏ **Tire Ashtray Collecting**
virgo.bsuvc.bsu.edu/~00jrkoenker/

❏ **Tried and True Trains**
www.tttrains.com/

❏ **U.S. Mint Stamps**
www.best.com/~mleon/usmints.html

❑ **Vexillology**
www.midcoast.com/~martucci/Vex.html

❑ **Virtual Flyshop**
www.flyshop.com/

❑ **Water Pressure Rockets**
www.isd.net/stobin/document/rockets.html

❑ **World Collectors Net**
www.worldcollectorsnet.com/

Home Page Advice

Folks on the Internet are anxious to tell you how to write your own home page on the Web.

❑ **6 Basic Rules of Web Design**
www.grantasticdesigns.com/5rules.html

❑ **Auditorial.com**
www.auditorial.com/

❑ **Avoiding Dithering Colors**
www.sirius.com/~industry/consider.html

❑ **BigNoseBird**
bignosebird.com/

❑ **Browser-Safe Color Palette**
www.lynda.com/hex.html

❑ **Color on the Web**
www.adobe.com/newsfeatures/palette/main.html

❑ **Creating a Succussful Web Page**
www.hooked.net/~larrylin/web.htm

❏ **EarthWeb Tutorials**
www.developer.com/classroom/tutorials/

❏ **Elements of Web Design**
builder.cnet.com/Graphics/Design/

❏ **Framing the Web**
webreference.com/dev/frames/

❏ **Free Web Page Design**
www.totalwebmaster.com/wd.html

❏ **Glassdog's Design-O-Rama**
www.glassdog.com/design-o-rama/
webdesign.html

❏ **Hands-on Training by DocOzone**
www.visi.com/~drozone/handson/

❏ **Home Page Design Tips**
public.tsu.ru/~boiko/koi-8/tips.shtml

❏ **Home Page Design Tenets**
www.bham.wednet.edu/homeswee.htm

❏ **Home Page Productions**
www.hpp.net/

❏ **Homepager's Web Site Resources**
www.homepagers.com/resour/htm1.html

❏ **Idiot's Guide to Making a Home Page**
www.voyager.co.nz/~bsimpson/html.htm

❏ **iSyndicate**
www.isyndicate.com/

❏ **Learn Web Publishing**
www.learnthenet.com/english/section/
webpubl.html

❑ **Make Some Noise**
builder.cnet.com/Authoring/Audio/

❑ **NCSA—A Beginner's Guide to HTML
Home Page**
www.ncsa.uiuc.edu/General/Internet/WWW
/HTMLPrimer.html

❑ **Net Ezy**
www.netezy.com/resources.htm

❑ **NetGuru**
www.netguru.com/

❑ **Photoshop Home Page**
es.rice.edu/projects/ravl/pshop

❑ **ReallyBig**
reallybig.com/default.shtml

❑ **SpiderSchool**
www.artswire.org/Artswire/spiderschool/
spider.htm

❑ **Ten Top Mistakes**
www.useit.com/alertbox/9706b.html

❑ **TipWorld**
www.tipworld.com/

❑ **Top Twelve Tips for Building Home Page**
www.indexstock.com/pages/hometip1.htm

❑ **Web Authoring FAQ**
www.htmlhelp.com/faq/html/all.html

❑ **Web Design Tips**
www.ochin.on.ca/webdesign/

❑ **Web Development Resources**
www.eborcom.com/webmaker/

❑ **Web Page Design**
werbach.com/web/page_design.html

❑ **Web Page Design Tips**
www.angelfire.com/nv/webpagedesign/

❑ **Web Site Garage**
www.websitegarage.com/

❑ **WebHome Improvement**
www.htmltips.com/

❑ **Webspawner**
www.webspawner.com/

❑ **WebSter's Dictionary**
www.goldendome.net/Tools/WebSter/

❑ **Yale Web Style Guide**
info.med.yale.edu/caim/manual/

Home Page Free Space

*These folks, for the most part, offer free disk
space and Web hosting services for your home
page. Some offer technical advice, and some
even make the page for you. Be aware also that
most sites limit page content, prohibiting, for
example, advertising or adult material.*

❑ **1-2-Free My Page**
www.1-2-free.com/mypage

❑ **AcmeCity**
www.acmecity.com/

❏ **Aid 4**
www.y4i.com/freeusa.html

❏ **Angelfire Communications**
www.angelfire.com/

❏ **B-City**
www.bcity.com/bcity

❏ **BraveNet**
www.bravenet.com/free_webtools_for_
webmasters.htm

❏ **Compu-Pro**
gocompupro.com/users/index.shtml

❏ **Crosswinds**
www.crosswinds.net/

❏ **Cybercities**
www.cybercities.com/

❏ **Cyberplace**
cyberplace.hypermart.net/index.htm

❏ **Free Web Space Providers Guide**
www.mediaport.org/~freepage/fpage1.htm

❏ **Free Webspace.Net**
www.freewebspace.net/

❏ **FreeYellow**
www.freeyellow.com/

❏ **GeoCities**
www.geocities.com

❏ **Homestead**
www.homestead.com/

❏ **HowdyNeighbor**
www.howdyneighbor.com/

❏ **Net Guide Free Web hosting**
www.netguide.com/Snapshot/
Archive?guide=internet&id=831

❏ **Nettaxi Online Communities**
www.nettaxi.com/

❏ **OneStop Network**
www.onestop.net/

❏ **Ostriches Online**
www.achiever.com/design/freehmpg.html

❏ **Personal Web Pages**
home.att.net/index.html

❏ **Space Ports**
www.spaceports.com/

❏ **Theglobe.com**
www.theglobe.com/

❏ **Tripod**
www.tripod.com/build/

❏ **Website Publishing and Hosting**
www.byop.com/

❏ **XOOM**
xoom.com/home/

Home Page—HTML Help Sites

Each of these sites offers information in its own way. Find the ones that are most helpful for you.

❑ **Ask Dr. Web**
www.zeldman.com/faq.html

❑ **Bare Bones HTML**
werbach.com/barebones/

❑ **Beginner's Guide to HTML**
www.web-nation.com/lessons/html-pri.htm

❑ **Beginner's Guide to HTML**
www.ncsa.uiuc.edu/General/Internet/
WWW/HTMLPrimer.html

❑ **Beyond the Bones of HTML**
www.avalon.net/~librarian/bones/

❑ **Composing Good HTML**
www.cs.cmu.edu/~tilt/cgh/

❑ **Dark Side of HTML**
www.best.com/~sem/dark_side/

❑ **David's FAQ html help**
www.dalleh.com/

❑ **Doctor HTML**
www2.imagiware.com/RxHTML/htdocs/
Explanation.html

❑ **How Do They Do That with HTML?**
www.nashville.net/~carl/htmlguide/

❑ **HTML Bad Style**
www.earth.com/bad-style/

❑ **HTML Clinic**
www.htmlclinic.com/

❑ **HTML Goodies**
www.htmlgoodies.com/

❏ **HTML Guide**
www.emerson.emory.edu/services/html/
html.html

❏ **HTML Help Central**
www.htmlhelpcentral.com/

❏ **HTML Quick Reference**
web.canlink.com/webdesign/htmlcard.html

❏ **Interactive HTML Tutorial for Beginners**
davesite.com/webstation/html/

❏ **Introduction to HTML**
www.cwru.edu/help/introHTML/toc.html

❏ **NetMechanic**
www.netmachanic.com/

❏ **WWW Help Page**
werbach.com/web/wwwhelp.html

Home Page Publicity

If tinkering with your home page is a favorite pastime, then check out these sites, all devoted to helping you publicize your home page. Some sites offer free service; others charge a fee. Some also explain how to hone your page so that it will be picked up by search engines.

❏ **101 Promotion Service**
www.kwik-link.com/c/promote.htm

❏ **AddURL**
aubmitit.linkexchnage.com/

❏ **Central Registry**
www.centralregistry.com/

❏ **Hit Man**
www.webthemes.com/hitman.html

❏ **Internet Promotions Megalist**
www.centralregistry.com/

❏ **Launch-it**
www.launch-it.com/

❏ **NetPost**
www.netpost.com/netpost2.html

❏ **PostMaster**
www.netcreations.com/postmaster/

❏ **Register It**
www.register-it.com/

❏ **Site Promoter**
www.sitepromoter.com/

❏ **Submit Blaster**
www.ansur.net/

❏ **Submit It!**
www.submit-it.com/

❏ **Submit to Search Engines and Directories**
www.aniota.com/~jwhite/submit.html

❏ **Virtual Promote**
www.virtualpromote.com/

❏ **WebStep Top 100**
www.mmgco.com/top100.html

Houses—Buying and Selling

Buying, Building, Selling. See also *Architecture.*

❏ **4 Sale by Owner**
www.byownersales.com/

❏ **ABC's of Real Estate**
www.realestateabc.com/

❏ **All About Home**
www.allabouthome.com/

❏ **Ask the Builder**
www.askbuild.com/

❏ **Buy-a-Farm**
www.buy-a-farm.com/

❏ **By Owner Online**
www.by-owner-ol.com/

❏ **E-Loan**
www.eloan.com/

❏ **Freddie Mac**
www.freddiemac.com/

❏ **Glossary of Real Estate and Mortgage Terms**
www.vamch.com/reinfo.html

❏ **Holiday Junction**
www.holidayjunction.com/

❏ **Home Inspection SuperSite**
www.inspectamerica.com/index.htm

❏ **Home Starter Kit**
www.homepath.com/hsp1.html

❏ **HomeNet**
www.netprop.com/

❏ **Homeowners Finance Center**
www.homeowners.com/

❏ **HomePath**
www.homepath.com/

❏ **Homes.com**
www.homes.com/

❏ **International Real Estate Digest**
www.ired.com/

❏ **Internet Design Center**
www.internetdesigncenter.com/

❏ **Internet Realty Network**
www.gorealty.com/contents.html

❏ **ListingLink**
listinglink.com/

❏ **Mortgage Calculators**
www.mortgage-net.com/calculators/

❏ **Mover Quotes**
moverquotes.com/

❏ **NewHomeSearch**
www.newhomesearch.com/

❏ **Open House America**
www.openhouse.net/

❑ **Quicken Mortgage**
www.quickenmortgage.com/

❑ **Realtor.com**
www.realtor.com/

❑ **Realty Advisor**
www.realtyadvisor.com/

❑ **Realty Locator**
www.realtylocator.com/

❑ **Relocate America**
www.nationwidehomes.com/

❑ **Relocation Central**
www.relocationcentral.com/

❑ **Rural Estate Network**
www.ruralspace.com/

❑ **The Home Buying Process**
www.interest.com/mortimer.html

❑ **The Mortgage Store**
www.mortgagestore.com/

❑ **Virtual Relocation**
www.virtualrelocation.com/

❑ **Welcome to the MLS**
www.wisconsinhomes.com/

Houses—Remodeling and Repairing

*Need some help with repairs around the house?
All kinds of folks are ready to offer assistance.*

❏ **BH & G Home Improvement Encyclopedia**
www.bhglive.com/homeimp/

❏ **Energy Outlet**
www.energyoutlet.com/

❏ **Fix-It**
begin.com/fixit/

❏ **HearthNet**
hearth.com/

❏ **Home Ideas**
www.homeideas.com/

❏ **Home Improvement and Repair**
www.hometime.com/

❏ **Home Improvement Highway**
www.csz.com/hih/

❏ **Home Improvement Tips**
www.housenet.com/

❏ **Home Lighting**
www.homelighting.com/

❏ **Homebuyer's Fair**
www.homefair.com/home/

❏ **Household Cyclopedia**
members.xoom.com/mspong/

❏ **HouseNet**
www.housenet.com/

❏ **ImproveNet**
www.improvenet.com/

Kitchen-Bath
www.kitchen-bath.com/

❑ **LivingHome**
www.livinghome.com/

❑ **Owners'Network**
www.owners.com/

❑ **Paint Estimator**
www.bhglive.com/homeimp/docs/
v0000041.htm

❑ **Remodeling Forum**
www.thathomesite.com/forums/remodel/

❑ **Remodeling Links and Resources**
www.contractorlocate.com/diy/remodeling/

❑ **Remodeling Online**
www.remodeling.hw.net/

❑ **This Old House**
www.pbs.org/wgbh/thisoldhouse/

❑ **Today's Homeowner**
www.todayshomeowner.com/repair/
index.html

❑ **Toolsource**
www.remodeling.hw.net/

❑ **True Value**
www.truevalue.com/

❑ **Whole House Remodeling**
www.bentyler.com/wholehouse.html

How To

There are many serious sites that offer comprehensive advice or instructions. Not here. These sites offer limited information on a limited topic, some serious and some frivolous. The titles here reflect what they offer.

❏ **Apply for U.S. Citizenship**
home.earthlink.net/~bobodonnell/apply.html

❏ **Awakening Your Child's Genius**
www.thelearninglink.org/itm00058.htm

❏ **Be Better Off a Year from Now**
www.ymcpa.com/article2.htm

❏ **Breakdance**
www.howtobreakdance.com/

❏ **Build a Frame Loom**
www.hallnet.com/build.html

❏ **Cite Internet Sources in Research Papers**
www.cgrg.ohio-state.edu/interface/
W96/page.html

❏ **Claim Your Unclaimed Money**
www.foundmoney.com/

❏ **Do CPR**
www.amherst.edu/~jaloduca/cpr.html

❏ **Find a Lost Friend**
www.lost-and-found.com/lfc/locate.html

❏ **Get the Exact Time**
tycho.usno.navy.mil

❏ **Get Your Way at the Auto Dealer**
www.edmunds.com/edweb/usedinfo/
contents.html

❏ **How to Change Your Motor Oil**
www.ehow.com/eHow/eHow/0,1053,11,00.
html?src=bre1

❏ **How to Choose the Right Dog**
www.digitaldog.com/choosing.html

❏ **How to Drive a Railway or Railroad
Locomotive**
www.geocities.com/picketfence/9549/

❏ **How to Escape a Boring Job?**
www.xs4all.nl/~hoefsmid/boring_j.htm

❏ **How to Paint the Interior of Your House**
idid.essortment.com/howtointerior_rvxy.htm

❏ **How to Prune Trees**
willow.ncfes.umn.edu/HT_prune/
PRUN001.HTM

❏ **How to Get Russian Fonts**
www.unn.ac.ru/rusfonts.htm

❏ **How to Guide the Blind**
www.dpa.org.sg/DPA/discond/gb.htm

❏ **Juggle**
www.jestdandy.com/howtojuggle.htm

❑ **Keep Your Blood Pressure Under Control**
www.coolware.com/health/medical_reporter/
hypertension.html

❑ **Learn a New Fact Each Day**
www.learningkingdom.com/press/coolfact/
coolfact.html

❑ **Learn2 Remove a Stain**
www.learn2.com/05/0513/0513.asp

❑ **Make a Kite**
www.interlog.com/~excells/kites/make.html

❑ **Make a Pie Crust**
www.teleport.com/~psyched/pie/crust.html

❑ **Make a Pop-up Card**
www.makersgallery.com/joanirvine/
howto.html

❑ **Make a Violin**
www.graffiti.it/stradivari/photostory/
storybrd.html

❑ **Make Vietnamese Noodle Soup**
www.best.com/~phohoa

❑ **Passport Services**
www.travel.state.gov/passport_services.html

❑ **Play Go**
www.webwind.com/go/goLes/goLes1.htm

❑ **Prepare for an Earthquake**
quake.usgs.gov/

❑ **Prevent the Spread of Weeds**
www.blm.gov/education/weeds/weed.html

❑ **Protect Yourself from Auto Theft**
www.watchyourcar.org/index2.html

❑ **Tombstone Rubbings**
www.amberskyline.com/treasuremaps/
t_stone.html

❑ **Unclog a Drain**
www.clickit.com/bizwiz/homepage/
plumber.htm

❑ **Use Fresh Culinary Herbs**
www.herbthyme.com/howtous.htm

❑ **Wolf Pup Adoption Center**
www.thewebbrawls.com/wolfpack/adopt.html

❑ **Write a Complaint Letter**
www.csag.cs.uiuc.edu/individual/pakin/
complaint

Humor

*Much humor on the Internet is funny indeed, but
a lot of it is simply terrible. We have tried to
present an inoffensive sampling.*

❑ **Argon Zark**
www.zark.com/front/hub.html

❑ **Art Faux Fine Art Gallery**
www.pcmagic.net/cpinckney/

❑ **Bob's Fridge Door**
www.bobsfridge.com/

❏ **British Comedy**
www.prairienet.org/britcom/

❏ **Calvin and Hobbes**
www.uexpress.com/ups/comics/ch/

❏ **Cartoon Network**
www.cartoonnetwork.com/wpt/index.html

❏ **Cartoon World!**
www.cet.com/~rascal/

❏ **Cathy**
www.uexpress.com/ups/comics/ca/

❏ **Center for the Easily Amused**
www.amused.com/

❏ **Chickenhead**
www.chickenhead.com/

❏ **Comedy Central**
www.comcentral.com

❏ **Comedy Films**
comedymovies.about.com/movies/
comedymovies/mbody.htm

❏ **Comedy Web**
www.comedyweb.co.uk/

❏ **Common Boundaries**
www.commonb.com/comics/

❏ **Crimson Empire**
www.starwars.com/crimson/index.html

❏ **Daily Muse**
www.cais.com/aschnedr/muse.htm

❏ **DC Comics**
www.dccomics.com/

❏ **Dilbert Zone**
www.dilbert.com/

❏ **Doonesbury**
www.doonesbury.com/

❏ **Funny**
www.funny.co.uk/

❏ **Funny Jokes**
www.twistedhumor.com/

❏ **Gibbleguts**
www.gibbleguts.com/frameset2.htm

❏ **Ha!**
www.hardyharhar.com/

❏ **Humor.com**
www.humor.com/

❏ **Humor Search**
www.humorsearch.com/

❏ **I Hate Computers**
extlab1.entnem.ufl.edu/IH8PCs/index.html

❏ **Internet Funny Pages**
www.its.bldrdoc.gov/%7Ebing/cartoons.html

❏ **Internet Squeegee Guy**
www.website1.com/squeegee/

❏ **Jokes.com**
www.jokes.com/

❑ **Jokes Magazine**
jokesmagazine.com/

❑ **Manic Media**
www.epgmedia.com/manic/openhtml

❑ **Not in My Backyard**
www.notinmybackyard.com/strips/

❑ **The Onion**
www.theonion.com/

❑ **Philosophical Humor**
www.u.arizona.edu/~chalmers/
phil-humor.html

❑ **Science Jokes**
www.xs4all.nl/~jcdverha/scijokes/

❑ **Short Attention Span**
www.amused.com/sass.html

❑ **Sick and Twisted Jokes**
www.sickjokes.about.com/comedy/
sickjokes/mbody.htm

❑ **Smile**
www.sacbee.com/smile/smile.html

❑ **Stress Relief Aquarium**
www.amused.com/fish.html

❑ **The Comedy Store**
www.comedystore.com/

❑ **The Comedy Underground**
www.comedyunderground.com/

❑ **Top Cow**
www.topcow.com/

I Can't Keep Staying Up All Night

If you enter one of these sites, you won't leave soon. Consider yourself warned.

❑ **Addicted to Stuff**
www.morestuff.com/index2.htm

❑ **After Dinner**
www.afterdinner.com/

❑ **Bingo Blitz**
www.worldvillage.com/bingo/index.html

❑ **Chains**
found.cs.nyu.edu/andruid/CHAINS.html

❑ **Cherry Coke Wall**
www.ccwall.com/

❑ **Cold Case**
www.coldcase.com/

❑ **Dear Abby**
www.uexpress.com/ups/abby/

❑ **Deoxyribonucleic Hyperdimension**
www.deoxy.org/index.htm

❑ **Function**
www.function.org/

❑ **History of the Mystery**
www.mysterynet.com/history/mystery/

❑ **HotAIR**
www.improb.com/

❏ **Infiltration**
www.infliltration.org/

❏ **Insomnia**
ccwf.cc.utexas.edu/~swilson/Insomnia.html

❏ **Interesting Ideas**
www.mcs.net/~billsw/home.html

❏ **Mystery Science Theater 3000**
www.scifi.com/mst3000/

❏ **Optical Illusions**
www.sandlotscience.com/

❏ **Random Links**
www.random.com/

❏ **Synthetic Journal**
www-personal.umich.edu/~rmutt/sj/
index.html

❏ **The Case**
www.thecase.com

❏ **Trivia Web**
www.trivia.net/

❏ **Web Soup**
sctest.cse.ucsc.edu/roth/WebSoup/

❏ **What They Meant to Say Was . . .**
www.carpedrm.com/wtmtsw.htm

Information You Probably Don't Need

But we include it anyway, just in case.

❏ **Advertising Graveyard**
www.zeldman.com/ad.html

❏ **Antics**
www.ionet.net/~rdavis/antics.shtml

❏ **Ask Mr. Bad Advice**
www.echonyc.com/~spingo/Mr.BA/

❏ **Billy Bob Teeth**
www.billybobteeth.com/

❏ **Bodyguard Home Page**
www.iapps.org/

❏ **Demotivation Posters**
www.cs.wustl.edu/~schmidt/
demotivation.html

❏ **HQ2O**
www.hq2o.com/

❏ **Online Surgery**
www.onlinesurgery.com/

❏ **Quitting with Style**
www.iquit.org/

❏ **Random Elizabethan Curse Generator**
www.tower.org/insult/insult.html

❏ **Shuffle Brain**
www.indiana.edu/~pietsch/

❏ **Skeptics Society**
www.skeptic.com/

❏ **Sleep Analysis**
www.swoon.com/dream/

❑ **Twinkies**
www.owlnet.rice.edu/~gouge/twinkies.html

❑ **Useless Knowledge**
www.uselessknowledge.com/

❑ **Wacky Patent of the Month**
colitz.com/site/wacky.htm

❑ **Zen Stories to Tell Your Neighbors**
www1.rider.edu/~suler/zenstory/
zenstory.html

International Trade

*Even novices can get info about international
commerce from the Internet.*

❑ **Europa**
europa.eu.int/index.htm

❑ **Global Commerce Link**
www.commerce.com/

❑ **Global Trade Center**
www.tradezone.com/welcome.html

❑ **Import-Export Portal**
www.fita.org/webindex.html

❑ **InfoManage**
www.infomanage.com/international/trade/

❑ **Internnational Business Forum**
www.ibf.com/

❑ **International Business Resources on
the WWW**
ciber.bus.msu.edu/busres/inttrade.htm

❏ **International Trade Administration**
www.ita.doc.gov/

❏ **International Trade Data Network**
www.itdn.net/

❏ **International Trade Fairs**
www.trade-fair.com/

❏ **International Trade Law**
www.spfo.unibo.it/spolfo/TRADE.htm

❏ **Internationalist**
www.internationalist.com/

❏ **Investigative Resources International**
www.lainet.com/factfind/

❏ **i-Trade**
www.i-trade.com/

❏ **The International Trade Journal**
www.tamiu.edu/itj/

❏ **Trade Compass**
www.tradecompass.com/

❏ **Trade Information Center**
tradeinfo.doc.gov/

❏ **Tradeport**
tradeport.org/

❏ **U.S. Census Bureau**
www.census.gov/ftp/pub/foreign-trade/www/

❏ **USATrade.gov**
www.usatrade.gov/

❏ **U.S. Court of International Trade**
www.uscit.gov/

❏ **U.S. International Trade Commission**
www.usitc.gov/

❏ **U.S. International Trade Statistics**
www.census.gov/foreign-trade/www/

❏ **U.S. Trade Representative**
www.ustr.gov/

❏ **World Trade Center**
www.worldtradecenter.org/

❏ **Worldclass Supersite**
web.idirect.com/~tiger/supersit.htm

Internet: Beginners
Start Here

Surf smarter. You won't feel like a newbie once you have perused some of these sites.

❏ **Beginners Central**
www.northernwebs.com/bc/

❏ **Best Internet Tutorials**
www.bgsu.edu/departments/tcom/
tutors2.html

❏ **Dummies Daily**
www.dummiesdaily.com/

❏ **Getting Started**
www.gettingstarted.net/

❏ **Internet 101**
www2.famvid.com/i101/

❏ **Internet Background and Basics**
www.refstar.com/internet/

❏ **Internet Dictionary**
www.oh-no.com/define.html

❏ **Internet Facts**
www.parallaxweb.com/interfacts.html

❏ **Internet FAQs**
www.boutell.com/faq/

❏ **Internet help Desk**
w3.one.net/~alward/

❏ **Internet in a Baby**
www.wideweb.com/baby

❏ **Internet Sampler**
www.net.org/is/WhatIsInternet.html

❏ **Jargon File**
beast.cc.emory.edu/Jargon30/JARGON.HTML

❏ **Learn the Net**
www.learnthenet.com/

❏ **Life on the Internet**
www.screen.com/start/welcome.html

❏ **Net Lingo**
www.netlingo.com/

❏ **Newbie Dome**
www.candleweb.net/newbie/

❏ **Newbie Net**
www.newbie.net/

❏ **Overview of the Web**
www.imagescape.com/helpweb/www/
oneweb.html

❑ **Sites for Internet Beginners**
venus.calstatela.edu/Training/newbie.htm

❑ **Starting Points for Internet Beginners**
www.acad.bg/beginner/beginner.html

❑ **The New User's Directory**
hcs.harvard.edu/~calvarez/newuser.html

❑ **Using and Understanding the Internet**
www.pbs.org/uti/begin.html

❑ **Welcome To Internet 101**
www2.famvid.com/i101/

❑ **WebNovice**
www.webnovice.com/

❑ **WhatIs**
whatis.com/

Internet Directories and Portals

Good starting places. Just about everything is listed, usually by category.

❑ **21st Century Network**
www.21net.com/index_n.htm

❑ **AllCampus**
www.allcampus.com/

❑ **AnyWho**
www.anywho.com/

❑ **Big Eye**
www.bigeye.com

❏ **Britannica Internet Guide**
www.britannica.com/

❏ **CNET**
www.cnet.com/

❏ **Daily Overlook**
www.thedaily.com/overlook.html

❏ **Essential Links**
www.el.com/

❏ **Galaxy**
www.einet.net/

❏ **GO.com**
www.go.com/WebDir/Computing/Internet/
Searching_and_exploring/Internet_directories

❏ **HotSheet**
www.tstimipreso.com/hotsheet/

❏ **Infomine**
lib-www.ucr.edu/Main.html

❏ **Infospace**
www.infospace.com/

❏ **LookSmart**
www.looksmart.com

❏ **Mining Company**
www.miningco.com/

❏ **My Look**
mylook.com/

❏ **NetGuide Live**
www.netguide.com/

❏ **Net Search**
home.netscape.com/home/
internet-search.html

❏ **Search Beat**
www.search-beat.com/

❏ **Snap**
www.snap.com/

❏ **Starting Point**
www.stpt.com/

❏ **TheCoolSite**
www.thecoolsite.com/Internet/Directories/

❏ **Third Voice**
www.thirdvoice.com/

❏ **Virtual Reference Desk**
www.refdesk.com/

❏ **Web Soup**
www.urus.net/WebSoup/

❏ **WebCrawler Select**
webcrawler.com/select/

❏ **Yahoo**
www.yahoo.com/

❏ **Yanoff's Internet Services**
www.spectracom.com/islist/

Internet Ethics

*These sites include everything from appropriate
behavior on the Internet to deep thoughts about
its implications for society.*

❏ **Code of Ethics for Internet E-Commerce**
emailausonline.com/au/auson/ethics.htm

❏ **Computers, Ethics, and Society**
www.wargaming.net/internet/61/
Computers_Ethics_Society.htm

❏ **Cyber Rights**
www.cpsr.org/cpsr/nii/cyber-rights/

❏ **Electronic Frontier Foundation**
www.eff.org/

❏ **Ethics and the Internet**
www.duke.edu/~wgrobin/ethics/

❏ **Ethics of Journalism on the Internet**
userwww.sfsu.edu/~sonlu/topic1.htm

❏ **Ethics Resources on the WWW**
www.ethics.ubc.ca/resources/

❏ **Internet Advertising Code of Ethics**
www.aap.es/ingles/CODINTIN.HTM

❏ **Internet Behavior and Ethics**
www.abacon.com/compsite/conversation/
netiquette.html

❏ **Internet Ethics and Etiquette**
www.ciolek.com/WWWVLPages/QltyPages/
QltyEtiq.html

❏ **Internet Ethics Organizations**
www.uncwil.edu/people/vetterr/CLASSES/
csc105-ss98/ethics2.html

❏ **Internet Society**
www.isoc.org/

❏ **LegalEthics: The Internet Ethics Site**
www.legalethics.com/index.html

❏ **Net Ethics**
www.netethique.com/

❏ **Netiquette Home Page**
www.albion.com/netiquette/index.html

❏ **Netiquette Primer**
jade.wabash.edu/wabnet/info/netiquet.htm

❏ **Selected Internet Ethics Resources**
www.unf.edu/library/guides/ethics.html

Internet: Everything You've Always Wanted to Know

Potpourri. There are always many Internet-related sites that are hard to categorize.

❏ **1001 Internet Tips**
www4.zdnet.com/pccomp/besttips/

❏ **Ask Dr. Internet**
promo.net/drnet/

❏ **Balkanization of the Web**
www.dsiegel.com/balkanization/

❏ **BrowserWatch**
browserwatch.iworld.com/

❏ **CERN Welcome**
www.cern.ch/

❏ **City of Bits**
www-mitpress.mit.edu/City_of_Bits

❑ ColorMix
www.colormix.com/

❑ Create Your Own Logo
www.webgfx.ch/

❑ Creative Good Help Pages
www.creativegood.com/help/index.html

❑ DLL Archive
solo.abac.com/dllarchive/index.html

❑ EarthCam
www.earthcam.com/

❑ Easter Egg Archive
www.eeggs.com/

❑ File Formats
www.learnthenet.com/english/html/
34filext.htm

❑ Global Internet Statistics
www.euromktg.com/globstats/

❑ Hipbone
www.conavigator.com/

❑ ICYouSee
www.ithaca.edu/library/Training/ICYouSee.
html#7

❑ Internet Archive
www.archive.org/

❑ Internet Channel
www.inch.com/index.html

❑ Internet Economy
www.internetindicators.com/

❑ **Internet Information Center**
www.Austria.Eu.Net/iic/

❑ **Internet Statistics**
lcweb.loc.gov/global/internet/inet-stats.html

❑ **Internet Web Text Index**
www.december.com/web/text/index.html

❑ **Net.Genesis**
www.netgen.com/

❑ **Press Questions to Tim Berners-Lee**
www.w3.org/People/Berners-Lee/FAQ.html

❑ **Ribbon Campaigns on the Internet**
gargaro.com/ribbons.html

❑ **SquareOne Technology**
www.squareonetech.com/

❑ **Survey Net**
www.survey.net/

❑ **The Rail**
www.therail.com/cgi-bin/station

❑ **TUCOWS**
www.tucows.com/

❑ **Virtual Tourist**
wings.buffalo.edu/world/

❑ **W3C**
www.w3.org/

❑ **Web Developer's Virtual Library**
wdvl.com/

❑ **Web Manage Technology**
www.webmanage.com/

❑ **Web Monkey**
www.hotwired.com/webmonkey/

❑ **Web Rings**
www.webring.org/

❑ **Web Standards Project**
www.webstandards.org/

❑ **Webopaedia**
webopedia.internet.com/

❑ **WebTrends**
www.webtrends.com/

❑ **World Wide Web Acronyms**
www.ucc.ie/info/net/acronyms/acro.html

❑ **World Wide Web Consortium**
www.w3.org/pub/WWW/

❑ **Yahoo What's New**
www.yahoo.cop/new

Internet Filters

Filter software can act as a barrier between children and inappropriate sites.

❑ **Clean Surf**
www.cleansurf.com/

❑ **Cyber Patrol**
www.cyberpatrol.com

❑ **Integrity Online**
www.integrityonline16.com/

❏ **Internet Filters**
www.solidoak.com/download.htm

❏ **Internet Lifeguard**
www.safesurf.com/lifegard.htm

❏ **Kid Safety**
www.ou.edu/ouopd/kidsafe/inet.htm

❏ **Net Nanny**
www.netnanny.com/

❏ **SafeSurf**
www.safesurf.com/

Internet Greeting Cards

Several sites let you send free electronic greeting cards, often complete with music, to friends online. The URL for the greeting card site will be waiting when the recipient picks up his or her e-mail.

❏ **123 Greetings**
www.123greetings.com/

❏ **1001 Postcards**
www.postcards.org/

❏ **AAAPostcards.com**
www.aaapostcards.com/

❏ **Absolutely Amazing Greeting Cards**
microimg.com/postcards/

❏ **Amercan Greetings**
www.americangreetings.com/

❏ **Audiocard.com**
www.audiocard.com/

❏ **Blue Mountain**
www1.bluemountain.com/

❏ **CardCentral**
www.cardcentral.net/weekly.htm

❏ **Cyber Greeting Cards**
www.cyber-greeting-cards.com/

❏ **E-Cards**
www.e-cards.com/site/

❏ **E-Greetings**
www.egreetings.com/e-products/m_main/
cgi/homepage

❏ **Electric Postcard**
postcards.www.media.met.edu/Postcards/

❏ **Hallmark**
www.hallmark.com/

❏ **MaxRacks**
www.maxracks.com/

❏ **Musical Greeting Cards**
www.zworks.com/forever/

❏ **Postcards from the Web**
homearts.com/postcard/00postf1.htm

❏ **Regards.com**
www.regards.com/

❏ **Send a Greeting**
www.sendgreeting.com/

❏ **Web Cards**
www.wbwebcards.com/

Internet History

Pick any site and it should be sufficient. But if the Internet is a passion, then by all means, take a look at several.

❏ **A Brief Hisory of the Internet**
info.isoc.org/internet-history/brief.html

❏ **A Little History of the World Wide Web**
www.w3.org/History.html

❏ **About the World Wide Web**
www.w3.org/WWW/

❏ **As We May Think**
www.ps.uni-sb.de/~duchier/pub/vbush/vbush.shtml

❏ **Brief History of the Internet and Related Networks**
info.isoc.org/internet-history/cerf.html

❏ **Classic RAND Papers on Packet Switching**
www.rand.org/publications/RM/baran.list.html

❏ **Community Memory**
memex.org/community-memory.html

❏ **Digital Time Capsule**
mitsloan.mit.edu/timecapsule/main.html

❏ **History of ARPANet**
www.dei.isep.ipp.pt/docs/arpa.html

❏ **History of the Internet**
www.internetvalley.com/intval.html

❏ **Hobbes Internet Timeline**
info.isoc.org/guest/zakon/Internet/History/
HIT.html

❏ **How the Internet Came to Be**
www.bell-labs.com/user/zhwang//vcerf.html

❏ **Internet and World Wide Web History**
www.elsop.com/wrc/h_web.htm

❏ **Internet Archive**
www.archive.org/

❏ **Internet Pioneers**
www.internet-history.org/

❏ **Nerds 201: A Brief History of the Internet**
www.pbs.org/opb/nerds2.0.1/

❏ **Net Hype**
jrowse.mtx.net/net/hype.html

❏ **NetHistory**
www.geocities.com/SiliconValley/2260/

❏ **PBS Life on the Internet Timeline**
www.pbs.org/internet/timeline/index.html

❏ **Roads and Crossroads of Internet History**
www.internetvalley.com/intvalold.html

❏ **Tim Berners-Lee**
www.w3.org/People/Berners-Lee

❏ **Usenet History**
www.vrx.net/usenet/history/

❏ **Web Origins and Beyond**
www.seas.upenn.edu/~lzeltser/WWW/

Internet Search Engines

No two search engines are alike. Each has its own attractions and method of presenting results. Try several. You will probably find two or three favorites for your everyday search needs.

❏ **Accufind**
www.accufind.com/

❏ **All-in-One**
www.albany.net/allinone/all1www.html/
#WWW

❏ **AltaVista**
www.altavista.com

❏ **Ask Jeeves**
www.ask.com/

❏ **Copernic.com**
www.copernic.com/

❏ **Deja News**
www.dejanews.com/

❏ **Direct Hit**
www.directhit.com/

❏ **Dogpile**
www.dogpile.com/

❏ **Easy Searcher**
www.easysearcher.com/home.html

❏ **Editorial Search**
www.opinion-pages.org/

❏ **Event Search**
www.ipworld.com/events/search.htm

❏ **Excite!**
www.excite.com/

❏ **Fast Search**
www.alltheweb.com/

❏ **Findspot**
www.findspot.com/

❏ **Forum One**
www.forumone.com/

❏ **Google**
www.google.com

❏ **GovBot**
ciir2.cs.umass.edu/Govbot/

❏ **HotBot**
www.hotbot.com/

❏ **Infoseek**
www.infoseek.com/

❏ **Internet Exploration**
www.amdahl.com/internet/

❏ **Mamma.com**
www.mamma.com/

❏ **Magellan**
www.mckinley.com

❏ **MetaCrawler**
www.go2net.com/search.html

❑ **NetSearcher**
www.searchinsider.com/

❑ **One Look Dictionary**
www.onelook.com/

❑ **Philosophy Research**
noesis.evansville.edu/

❑ **SearchIQ**
www.searchiq.com/

❑ **SearchPower.com**
www.searchpower.com/

❑ **SportSearch**
www.sportsearch.com/

❑ **WebCrawler**
www.webcrawler.com/

Internet Security and Privacy

Both expert and amateur Interent users are concerned about security leaks and privacy erosion on the Internet. These issues are addressed repeatedly by everyone from sociologists to computer scientists. We list some of the easy-to-read sites here.

❑ **Center for Internet Security**
www.cisecurity.org/

❑ **Computer Security Information**
www.alw.nih.gov/Security/security.html

❑ **Cookie Central**
www.cookiecentral.com

❏ **Counterpane Internet Security**
www.counterpane.com/

❏ **Electronic Privacy Information Center**
epic.org/

❏ **Firewalls and Security**
www.digitex.cc/Products/firewalls.html

❏ **Georgetown Internet Privacy Policy Study**
www.msb.edu/faculty/culnanm/
gippshome.html

❏ **Internet Firewalls**
www.interhack.net/pubs/fwfaq/

❏ **Internet Privacy Coalition**
www.crypto.org/

❏ **Internet Privacy Home Page**
www.osu.edu/units/law/swire1/pspriv.htm

❏ **Internet Privacy Sites**
www.cs.buffalo.edu/~milun/privacy.html

❏ **Internet Privacy: A Public Concern**
www.research.att.com/~lorrie/pubs/
networker-privacy.html

❏ **Internet Scambusters**
www.scambusters.org/index.html

❏ **Internet Security Issues and Answers**
www.alw.nih.gov/Security/security.html

❏ **Junkbusters**
www.junkbusters.com/

❏ **Pretty Good Privacy Presentation**
www.stanford.edu/group/tdr-security/
PGP-Demo/index.htm

❏ **Privacy Pages**
www.orlandomaildrop.com/privacy.html

❏ **Protecting Your Internet Privacy**
cc.uoregon.edu/privacy.html

❏ **SonicWALL**
www.sonicwall.com/

❏ **TRUSTe**
www.etrust.org/

❏ **Understanding Net Users' Attitudes About Online Privacy**
www.research.att.com/projects/privacystudy/

❏ **WWW Security FAQs**
www.w3.org/Security/Faq/www-security-faq.html

Internet Service Providers

We will not list all the ISPs who offer their services; that is what these comprehensive sites do.

❏ **Directory of ISPs**
thedirectory.org/index.sht

❏ **Internet Access Providers Metalist**
www.hervison.com/herbison/iap_meta_list.html

❏ **ISP Finder**
www.cleansurf.com/

❏ **NetAccess Worldwide**
www.netalert.com/

❏ **The List: ISPs**
thelist.iworld.com/

❏ **Ultimate Guide to ISPs**
www.cnet.com/Content/Reviews/Compare/IS

Internet Site Makers and Designers

Want to see how the pros do it? Check out the sites these designers have made for themselves. Then check out the sites for their clientele.

❏ **4site**
4site.co.il/

❏ **47Jane**
www.47jane.com/

❏ **A List Apart**
www.alistapart.com/

❏ **Accent Design**
www.accentdesign.com/

❏ **Adjacency**
www.adjacency.com/

❏ **Adscape**
www.adscape.com/

❏ **Aristotole**
www.aristotle.net/design

❏ **Barns Designs**
www.barnsdesigns.co.uk/

❏ **Blue Cat Design**
www.bluecatdesign.com/

❏ **Blueberry**
www.blueberry.co.uk/

❑ **Brody**
www.brodynewmedia.som

❑ **Chman**
www.chman.com/

❑ **Curry Design**
www.currydesign.com/

❑ **Dahlin Smith White**
www.dsw.com

❑ **Desing Project**
design-agency.com/project/

❑ **EasyNet France**
www.easynet.fr

❑ **Egomedia**
www.egomedia.com

❑ **El Diablo Web Works**
www.eldiablowebworks.com/

❑ **Endeavour Page Makers**
www.pagemakers.com.au/index.php

❑ **Evolve Internet Design Solutions**
www.eids.co.uk/

❑ **EYE4U**
www.eye4u.com/

❑ **Fire Engine Red**
www.enginered.com/

❑ **Funkysites**
www.funkysites.co.uk/

❑ **Gabocorp**
www.gabocorp.com/

❏ **Giant Step**
www.giantstep.com/

❏ **Green Ant**
www.greenant.com.au/

❏ **Hi-D**
www.hi-d.com/

❏ **I2F**
www.i2f.org/

❏ **Ignition**
www.ignitiondesign.com/index.html

❏ **Ingram Labs**
www.ingramlabs.com/

❏ **Internet Professional Publishers**
www.ippa.org/

❏ **Iowa Web Design**
iowawebdesign.com/foyer.htm

❏ **Jiong**
www.jiong.com/

❏ **John Hersey**
www.hersey.com/

❏ **Juxt Interactive**
www.juxtinteractive.com/

❏ **K2 Design**
www.k2design.com/

❏ **Magnet Interactive**
www.magnet.com/

❏ **Metrolab Design**
www.metrolab.co.nz/

❏ **NetArchitects**
www.netarchitects.com/

❏ **Ninth Degree**
www.ninthdegree.com/default.asp?o=x

❏ **Oden**
www.odenvision.com/

❏ **Off the Page Productions**
www.offthepage.com/

❏ **Organic Online**
www.organic.com/

❏ **OS Web Creations**
www.os-web.com/

❏ **Ozark Showcase Web Designs**
www.ozarkwebdesign.com/

❏ **P2 Output**
www.p2output.com/

❏ **Plexus Web Creations**
www.plexusweb.com/

❏ **Promi Angeli**
www.primo.com/

❏ **Project Cool Media**
www.projectcool.com/

❏ **Prophet Communications**
www.prophetcomm.com/

❏ **Robbie de Villiars Design**
robbie.com/

❏ **Razorfish**
www.razorfish.com/

❏ **Richter Internet Site Designs**
www.megsinet.com/auzzii

❏ **Second Story**
www.secondstory.com/

❏ **Shadowmaker**
www.shadowboxer.com/

❏ **Sharp Services**
www.sharp-ideas.com/sharp.html

❏ **Siteline**
www.siteline.com/

❏ **Souldanse Digital Design**
www.souldanse.com/

❏ **Speared Peanut**
www.spearedpeanut.com/

❏ **Studio 1**
www.studio1.com.au/penstrokes/

❏ **Superbad**
www.superbad.com

❏ **Systems Alliance**
www.systemsalliance.com/index.cfm

❏ **Talbot Design**
www.talbotdesign.com/

❏ **Taylor and Pond**
www.taylorpond.com/

❏ **The Net Company**
www.thenetcompany.co.uk/

❏ **Turtle Design**
www.turtledesign.com/

❏ **Twelve Point Rule**
www.fusebox.com/

❏ **Verso**
www.verso.com/

❏ **Virtual Light Media**
www.virtuallightmedia.com/

❏ **Vivid Studios**
www.vivid.com/

❏ **VolumeOne**
www.volumeone.com/

Internet Webmasters

If you want to be a webmaster, or just wonder what they do, these sites supply plenty of information.

❏ **20 Tips for Mac Webmasters**
www.clearway.com/team/clearway/
mac-web-tips/home.html

❏ **Fade In, Fade Out**
builder.com/Authoring/MoreStupid/ss01.html

❏ **International Webmasters Association**
www.irwa.org/

❏ **Professor Pete's Webmastering 301**
www.professorpete.com/

❏ **Webmaster Seminars**
www.webmasterseminars.com/

❏ **Webmaster's Guide to Search Engines**
searchenginewatch.com/wgtse.htm

❏ **Webmaster's Notebook**
www.cio.com/fourms/intranet/notebook.html

❏ **Webmaster Association**
www.stars.com/Internet/Web/Associations.
html

❏ **Webmastery**
www.nothing.com/webmastery/

❏ **Webmaster Central**
webvivre.hypermart.net/

❏ **Webmaster International**
www.webmasterint.com/index5.htm

❏ **Webmaster Reference Library**
www.webreference.com/

❏ **Webmaster Station**
www.exeat.com/index.shtml

❏ **Webmaster's Color Lab**
www.visibone.com/colorlab/

Internships

*We hope this list is helpful. However, most peo-
ple get internships locally through networking.*

❏ **Akron Zoo Internships**
www.akronzoo.com/intern.asp

❏ **American Society of Magazine Editors**
www.asme.magazine.org/asme_internships/

❏ **Best Bets for Internships Abroad**
www.cie.uci.edu/iop/internsh.html

❏ **Center for Museum Studies**
museumstudies.si.edu/

❏ **Collegegrad Internship Postings**
www.collegegrad.com/internships/

❏ **Holocaust Museum Internships**
www.ushmm.org/internship.htm

❏ **Internships and Fieldwork Nationwide**
minerva.acc.viginia.edu/~career/intern.html

❏ **Internships.com**
www.internships.com/

❏ **Internships Directory**
www.feminist.org/911/internship/
internship.html

❏ **InternshipPrograms.com**
www.internshipprograms.com/

❏ **Internships Tokyo**
jintern.com/

❏ **Lands' End Internships**
de.landsend.com/

❏ **Medical Internships**
www.westga.edu/~coop/joblinks/subject/
medicalinternships.html

❑ **Mighty Internships**
www.daily.umn.edu/~mckinney/

❑ **National Internships Online**
www.internships.com/

❑ **Paid Student Internships in Asia**
www.interninasia.com/

❑ **PBS Jobs and Internships**
www.pbs.org/insidepbs/jobs/

❑ **Rising Star Internships**
www.rsinternships.com/

❑ **Small Business Administration Internships**
www.sba.gov/pmi

❑ **Summer Jobs, Internships**
www.jobweb.org/catapult/jintern.htm

❑ **Television Student Internships**
www.moviebytes.com/mb_contest_detail.cfm?contestnumber=1

❑ **The Heritage Foundation**
www.heritage.org/internships/

❑ **Tripod Internships**
www.tripod.com/explore/jobs_career/internships.html

❑ **Ubiquity Environmental Internships**
www.geocities.com/RainForest/8974/env7.htm

❑ **U.S. State Department Internships**
www.state.gov/www/careers/rinterncontents.html

❑ **Washington Center Internships**
www.twc.edu/

❑ **Zentropy Interactive, Inc.**
www.zentropy.com

Java

Okay, you've heard about it. But just what is it? And how can you use it? These sites tell all.

❑ **Absolute Beginner's Guide to Java**
www.fireflysoftware.com/javabeginner/

❑ **Brewing Java: A Tutorial**
metalab.unc.edu/javafaq/javatutorial.html

❑ **Club Java**
rendezvous.com/java/

❑ **Java Coffee Break**
www.javacofeebreak.com

❑ **ColorCenter**
www.hidaho.com/colorcenter/

❑ **Digital Espresso**
www.mentorsoft.com/DE/

❑ **Gamelan**
www.gamelan.com/

❑ **Introduction to Java**
www.ibm.com/java/education/intro/
courseoptions.htm

❑ **Java Arcade**
members.aol.com/edhobbs/applets/

❏ **Java FAQ Archives**
www-net.com/java/faq/

❏ **Java FAQs**
java.sun.com/products/jdk/faq.html

❏ **Java Games and Puzzles Gallery**
thinks.com/games/

❏ **Java Home Page**
java.sun.com/

❏ **Java Optimization**
www.cs.cmu.edu/~jch/java/optimization.html

❏ **Java Programmers FAQ**
www.afu.com/javafaq.html

❏ **Java Readings and Resources**
www.iat.unc.edu/guides/irg-42.html

❏ **JavaShareware.com**
www.javashareware.com/

❏ **Java Security**
www-swiss.ai.mit.edu/~jbank/javapaper/
javapaper.html

❏ **Java Tutorial**
java.sun.com/nav/read/Tutorial/

❏ **JavaSoft Home Page**
java.sun.com/

❏ **Java World Magazine**
www.javaworld.com/

❏ **Kneedeep in Java**
rummelplatz.uni-mannheim.de/~skoch/
javatut kneedeep.htm

❏ **Making Sense of Java**
www.disordered.org/Java-QA.html

❏ **Presenting Java**
www.december.com/works/java.html

Journalism

Journalism sites range from resources for getting the story to staunch defenses for the right to report the story.

❏ **CNN Search**
www.cnn.com/SEARCH/index.html

❏ **Committee to Protect Journalists**
www.cpj.org/

❏ **Digital Journalist**
dirckhalstead.org/

❏ **Experts directory**
www.experts.com/

❏ **Experts, Authorities, and Spokespersons**
www.yearbooknews.com/

❏ **Freedom Forum**
www.freedomoforum.org/

❏ **Internet Newsroom**
www2.dgsys.com/~editors/

❏ **Journalism Education Association**
www.jea.org/

❏ **Journalism History**
www.mediahistory.com/journ.html

❏ **Mediamatic Index**
www.mediamatic.nl/index.html

❏ **National Press Club**
npc.press.org/

❏ **Native Americans Journalists Association**
www.medill.nwu.edu/naja/

❏ **Online Journalism Review**
www.ojr.org/

❏ **Photojournalist's Coffee House**
www.intac.com/~jdeck/index2.html

❏ **Plesser Associates**
www.plesser.com/

❏ **Pulitzer Prizes**
www.pulitzer.org/

❏ **Society of Environmental Journalists**
www.sej.org/

❏ **Spot for Copyeditors**
www.theslot.com/

❏ **The Journalistic Resources Page**
www.markovits.com/journalism/

Kid Stuff

We could fill this whole book with nothing but kid sites. Some are educational, but most are just plain fun. Here are the best picks.

❏ **10-Minute Bedtime Tour**
www.hamstertours.com/

❑ **Ask Dr. Universe**
www.wsu.edu/DrUniverse

❑ **Bonus**
www.bonus.com/

❑ **ChaosKids**
chaoskids.com/

❑ **Chuckle Corner**
www.lyfe.freeserve.co.uk/kidspage.htm

❑ **Club-Z**
www.club-z.com/

❑ **Cool Science for Curious Kids**
www.hhmi.org/coolscience/

❑ **Dinosauer Eggs**
www.quaker-dinoeggs.com/

❑ **Kid's Castle**
www.kidscastle.si.edu/

❑ **Kid's Almanac**
kids.infoplease.com/

❑ **Kids @ nationalgeographic.com**
www.nationalgeographic.com/kids/

❑ **Kids Space**
www.kids-space.org/

❑ **Kid's Stuff!**
www.infostuff.com/kids/

❑ **Lego Mindstorm**
www.legomindstorms.com

❑ **Lego**
www.lego.com/

❑ **Lemonade Stand**
www.littlejason.com/lemonade/

❑ **Mr. Rogers' Neighborhood**
www.pbs.org/rogers/

❑ **Mudball**
www.halcyon.com/kat/mudball.htm

❑ **National Spelling Bee**
www.spellingbee.com/

❑ **Nickelodeon**
www.nick.com

❑ **Non-Stick Looney Page**
www.nonstick.com/

❑ **Planet Troll**
www.troll.com/

❑ **Rare Kids Games**
www.rarekids.com/games/

❑ **Sandlot Science**
www.sandlotscience.com/

❑ **Shooter's Doghouse**
www.shooterdog.com/

❑ **Sports Illustrated for Kids**
www.sikids.com/

❑ **Sticker World**
www.ctw.org/stickerworld/

❑ **Stories to Grow By**
www.storiestogrowby.com/

❑ **T Rex**
www.imax.com/t-rex

❑ **SuperKids Educational Software**
www.superkids.com/

❑ **Theodore Tugboat**
www.cochran.com/theodore/

❑ **Willie Wonka**
www.wonka.com/Home/wonka_home.html

❑ **Woogle.net**
www.woogle.net/

❑ **World Kids**
www.worldkids.com/

❑ **Yahooligans**
www.yahooligans.com/

❑ **Yeeeoww!**
www.yeeeoww.com/

❑ **Zoom Dinosaurs**
www.zoomdinosaurs.com/

Law—Forensic Science

Forensic science means "science as it relates to law"—usually the science involved in solving a crime.

❑ **American Academy of Forensic Psychology**
www.abfp.com/

❑ **American Society of Forensic Odontology**
asfo.org/

□ **Computer Forensics**
www.forensics.com/

□ **Forensic Entomology**
www.forensic-entomology.com/

□ **Forensic Links**
www.see-incorp.com/links.html

□ **Reddy's Forensic Home Page**
haven.ios.com/~nyrc/homepage.html

Law—General

*Need help with legal research? Just need help?
Legal matters, large and small, are addressed
on many sites.*

□ **Affordable Divorce Law**
www.divorce-forms.co.uk/

□ **American Bar Association**
www.abanet.org/home.html

□ **Anatomy of a Murder**
tqd.advanced.org/2760/

□ **Bazelon Center for Mental Health Law**
www.bazelon.org/

□ **Class Action Litigation Information**
www.classactionlitigation.com/

□ **Crime Statistics**
www.ojp.usdoj.gov/bjs/

□ **Critical Criminology**
sun.soci.niu.edu/~critcrim/

□ **Divorce Law: Free Legal Information**
family-law.freeadvice.com/divorce_law/

❑ **DivorceNet**
www.divorcenet.com/

❑ **Dumb Laws**
www.dumblaws.com/

❑ **Employment Law Resource Center**
www.ahipubs.com/

❑ **Famous American Trials**
www.law.umkc.edu/faculty/projects/Ftrials/
ftrials.htm

❑ **Federal Judicial Center**
www.fjc.gov/

❑ **FedLaw**
www.legal.gsa.gov/

❑ **Hieros Gamos**
www.hg.org/

❑ **Immigration Lawyers on the Web**
ilw.com/

❑ **International Constitutional Law**
www.uni-wuerzburg.de/law/index.html

❑ **Justice Information Center**
www.ncjrs.org/

❑ **Law Engine**
www.fastsearch.com/law/

❑ **Law Forum**
www.lawforum.net/

❑ **Law News Network**
www.lawnewsnetwork.com/

❑ **Law.com**
www.law.com/

❏ **LawGuru**
www.lawguru.com/

❏ **LawWorld**
www.lawworld.com/

❏ **Legal Information Institute**
www.law.cornell.edu/

❏ **Litigation Site**
www.ljx.com/litigation/

❏ **Mediation Information and Resource Center**
www.mediate.com/

❏ **National Association For Community Mediation**
www.nafcm.org/

❏ **National Consumer Law Center**
www.consumerlaw.org/

❏ **Police Dogs**
www.policek9.com/

❏ **Prairie Law**
prairielaw.com/

❏ **Southern Poverty Law Center**
www.splcenter.org/

❏ **The Journal of Online Law**
www.wm.edu/law/publications/jol/

❏ **U.S. Supreme Court Decisions**
supct.law.cornell.edu/supct/

❏ **United States Code**
www4.law.cornell.edu/uscode/

Law—Intellectual Property

Intellectual property is of particular interest to users of the Internet.

❏ **Cyber Law Centre**
www.cyberlawcentre.org.uk/

❏ **Free Trade Area for the Americas**
www.cptech.org/pharm/belopaper.html

❏ **Intellectual Property Center**
www.ipcenter.com/

❏ **Intellectual Property Data Collections**
ipdl.wipo.int/

❏ **Intellectual Property Law Server**
www.intelproplaw.com/

❏ **Intellectual Property Law Web Server**
www.patents.com/

❏ **Intellectual property: Copyrights, Trademarks, and Patents**
www.brint.com/IntellP.htm

❏ **Journal of Intellectual Property Law**
www.lawsch.uga.edu/~jipl/

❏ **Patent, Trademark, Copyright World**
www.ptcworld.com/

❏ **U.S. Intellectual Property for Non-Lawyers**
www.fplc.edu/tfield/order.htm

Maps

Most of the maps offered by these sites are useful, and some are even beautiful. But the handiest sites are the ones that draw a map to your specifications. Print it out, and start your trip.

❏ **Air Quality Mapping**
www.epa.gov/airnow/

❏ **Airport Maps**
www.thetrip.com/airport/

❏ **Antique Map Fair**
www.AntiqueMaps.co.uk/

❏ **Applied Geographics**
www.appgeo.com/~agi1/agitop.htm

❏ **Area Accurate Map**
www.webcom.com/bright/petermap.html

❏ **Atlas of Cyberspace**
www.cybergeography.com/

❏ **Census Bureau Digital Map Database**
tiger.census.gov/

❏ **Color Landform Map of the U.S.**
fermi.jhuapl.edu/states/states.html

❏ **DeLorme Maps**
www.delorme.com/

❏ **Etak**
www.etak.com/

❏ **Graphic Maps**
www.graphicmaps.com/graphic_maps.html

❏ **Historical Atlas of the 20th Century**
www.erols.com/mwhite28/20centry.htm

❏ **Historical Maps of the United States**
www.lib.utexas.edu/Libs/PCL/
Map_collection/histus.html

❏ **History of Cartography**
www-map.lib.umn.edu/history_of_
cartography.html

❏ **International Maps**
www.galaxymaps.com/

❏ **Library of Congress Map Collections**
memory.loc.gov/ammem/gmdhtml/
gmdhome.html

❏ **Lycos RoadMaps**
www.lycos.com/roadmap.html

❏ **MapBlast**
www.mapblast.com/

❏ **MapQuest**
www.mapquest.com/

❏ **Maps.com**
www.maps.com/

❏ **Maps of the Solar System**
maps.jpl.nasa.gov/

❏ **Maps in the News**
www-map.lib.umn.edu/news.html

❏ **Maps on Us**
www.mapsonus.com/

❏ **National Geographic Map Machine**
www.etak.com/

❏ **Open World City Guides**
www.libs.uga.edu/darchive/hargrett/maps/
maps.html

❏ **Rand McNally**
www.randmcnally.com/home/

❏ **Rare Map Collection**
www.libs.uga.edu/darchive/hargrett/maps/
maps.html

❏ **Road Map Collectors of America**
www.roadmaps.org/

❏ **Subway Maps**
www.libs.uga.edu/darchive/hargrett/maps/
maps.html

❏ **Thomas Brothers Mapping**
www.thomas.com/

❏ **TopoZone**
www.topozone.com/

❏ **U.S. Gazeteer**
www.census.gov/cgi-bin/gazetteer

❏ **Volcanic Maps**
www.geo.mtu.edu/volcanoes/world.html

❏ **Washington DC Sightseeing Map**
sc94.ameslab.gov/TOUR/tour.html

❏ **World City Maps**
www.lib.utexas.edu/Libs/PCLMap_
collection/world_cities.html

❑ **World of Maps**
www.worldofmaps.com/

❑ **Xerox PARC MapWeb Server**
pubweb.parc.xerox.com/

Mathematics

Tricks and tips and help with math.

❑ **Algebra Online**
www.algebra-online.com/

❑ **Ask Dr. Math**
forum.swarthmore.edu/dr.math/

❑ **Bamdad's Math Comics**
www.csun.edu/~hcmth014/comics.html

❑ **Brain Exerciser**
www.math.tau.ac.il./~puzne/gif/brain.html

❑ **Brain Teasers**
www.eduplace.com/math/brain/index.html

❑ **Dave's Math Tables**
www.sisweb.com/math/tables.htm

❑ **E-Math**
e-math.ams.org/

❑ **Exploring Your Future in Math and Science**
www.cs.wisc.edu/~karavan/afl/home.html

❑ **Fantastic Math Tricks**
www.angelfire.com/me/marmalade/
mathtips.html

❏ **Gomath.com**
www.gomath.com/

❏ **Harcourt Brace Math Glossary**
www.harcourtschool.com/glossary/math/

❏ **Interactive Math**
tqd.advanced.org/2647/index.html

❏ **Interactive Mathematics Miscellany and Puzzles**
www.cut-the-knot.com/

❏ **Inverse Symbolic Calculator**
www.cecm.sfu.ca/projects/ISC/

❏ **Math Art Gallery**
www-math.sci.kun.nl/math/knopen/
art_gallery.html

❏ **Math Baseball**
www.funbrain.com/math/

❏ **Math Forum**
forum.swarthmore.edu/

❏ **Math Homework Help**
www.erols.com/bram/column2.html

❏ **Math in Daily Life**
www.learner.org/exhibits/dailymath/

❏ **Math League Help Topics**
www.mathleague.com/help/help.htm

❏ **Mathematician Trading Cards**
www.bulletproof.org/math/default.asp

❏ **MathSoft**
www.mathsoft.com/

❑ **Mega-Mathematics**
www.cs.uidaho.edu/~casey931/
mega-math/menu.html

❑ **Monster Math**
www.lifelong.com/CarnivalWorld/
MonsterMath/MonMathHP.html

❑ **Ridiculously Enhanced Pi Page**
www.exploratorium.edu/learning_studio/pi/

❑ **WebMath**
www.webmath.com/

Miscellaneous

Don't know where to put these sites, but they are too good to pass up.

❑ **Alcatraz**
www.nps.gov/alcatraz/

❑ **Broken Plank**
www.profiles.nlm.nih.gov/

❑ **Caricature Zone**
www.magixl.com/

❑ **Circlemakers**
www.circlemakers.org/

❑ **Cynic's Sanctuary**
www.amz.com/cynic/

❑ **Despair, Inc.**
www.despair.com/

❑ **Estimated IQs of the Greatest Geniuses**
home8.swipnet.se/~w-80790/Index.htm

❏ Fading Ad Campaign
www.frankjump.com/

❏ Fake Food
www.faxfoods.com/

❏ Fifty Things Worth Saving
www.fiftythings.com/

❏ Grass-Roots Heroes
www.grass-roots.org/

❏ Half a Cow
www.halfacow.com/

❏ Her Majesty's Prison Service
www.hmprisonservice.gov.uk/

❏ I Thee Web
hollywoodandvine.com/Itheeweb/

❏ Ice Trek
www.icetrek.org/

❏ Kvetch
www.kvetch.com/index.html

❏ Laura's NYC Tales
www.laurasnyctales.com/

❏ Life Raft
www.liferaft.com/

❏ Mystery of the Day
www.mysteries.com/

❏ Name That Candybar
www.sci.mus.mn.us/sln/tf/c/crosssection/
namethatbar.html

❑ **New York Underground**
www.nationalgeographic.com/features/97/
nyunderground/index.html

❑ **NYCabbie**
www.nycabbie.com/

❑ **Odd Facts**
www.telacommunications.com/misc/facts.htm

❑ **Open Diary**
www.opendiary.com/

❑ **Pogo Sticks**
www.hvnet.com/pogoplaza/

❑ **Professional Butlers**
www.butlersguild.com/

❑ **Sneaker Nation**
sneaker-nation.com/

❑ **Spizzerinctum**
www.mcs.net/~kvj/spizz.html

❑ **Su Tzu's Chinese Philosophy Page**
mars.superlink.net/fsu/

❑ **The 80s Server**
www.80s.com/

❑ **Traffic Jam Cure**
www.eskimo.com/~billb/amateur/traffic/
seatraf.html

❑ **Vanity License Plates**
www.vanity-plates.com/

❑ **Wealthiest Americans**
www.americanheritage.com/98/oct/
40index.htm

❑ **World Wide Cemetery**
www.interlog.com/~cemetery/

Movies

*If movies are your passion, or even if they're not,
you can find out anything about them on the
Internet. This long list is just a small subset of
what is available.*

❑ **AAAFilm**
www.aaafilm.com/

❑ **AFI's 100 Years...100 Movies**
www.afionline.org/100movies/

❑ **American Movie Classics**
www.amctv.com/

❑ **CineMedia**
ptd15.afionline.org/CineMedia/

❑ **Classic Film Noir**
www.moviesunlimited.com/filmnoir.htm

❑ **Cult Films**
sepnet.com/rcramer/tv.htm

❑ **Dermatology in the Cinema**
www.skinema.com/

❑ **Film Scouts**
www.filmscouts.com/

❏ **FilmFour**
www.filmfour.com

❏ **Film History by Decade**
www.filmsite.org/filmh.html

❏ **filmmag.com**
www.filmmag.com/

❏ **Film Noir Films**
www.filmsite.org/filmnoir.html

❏ **Flicker**
www.sirius.com/~sstark

❏ **Former Child Star Central**
members.tripod.com/~former_child_star/

❏ **From Script to Screen**
fromscript2screen.com/

❏ **Hitchcock Page**
www.primenet.com/~mwc/

❏ **Hollywood Archeology**
www.echonyc.com/~hwdarch/

❏ **IMAX**
www.imax.com/home.shtml

❏ **Internet Movie Database**
www.imdb.com

❏ **Iowa Independent Film and Video Festival**
www.uni.edu/~martin/iifv.html

❏ **Loew's Cineplex**
www.theatres.sre.sony.com/

❏ MGM
www.mgmua.com/

❏ Miramax
www.miramax.com/

❏ Movie Bloopers Online
www.moviebloopers.com/

❏ Movie Posters
www.musicman.com/mp/posters.html

❏ Movie Scripts Online
www.geocities.com/Hollywood/7024/

❏ Moviefone
www.moviefone.com/

❏ Movies.com
movies.go.com/

❏ New York International Independent Film and Video Festival
www.nyfilmvideo.com/

❏ Ohio Independent Film Festival
www.ohiofilms.com/

❏ Quotes from the Movies
members.tripod.com/adm/popup/roadmap.shtml

❏ Silent Movies
www.cs.monash.edu.au/~pringle/silent/

❏ Small Movies
www.city-net.com/~fodder/

❑ **SoYou Wanna Make a Low-Budget Movie?**
www.soyouwanna.com/site/syws/
makemovie/makemovie.html

❑ **Teen Movie Critic**
www.dreamagic.com/roger/teencritic.html

❑ **The Complete History of the Discovery of Cinematography**
www.precinemahistory.net/

❑ **The Movie Mom**
www.moviemom.com/

❑ **The Movie Posters Archive**
anubis.science.unitn.it/services/movies/

❑ **The Ultimate Movie Clips**
www.ultimatemovieclips.com/

❑ **Useless Movie Quotes**
members.tripod.com/umq/umq.htm

Multimedia Resources

Here are sites that describe multimedia technology and/or sell a multimedia product.

❑ **Byron Preiss Multimedia**
www.byronpreiss.com/

❑ **Macromedia**
www.macromedia.com/

❑ **MPEG Resources**
www.mpeg.org/index.html/

❑ **Multimedia Authoring Web**
www.mcli.dist.maricopa.edu/authoring/

❏ **Multimedia Information Sources**
viswiz.gmde.de/MultimediaInfo/

❏ **Multimedia Search**
www.scour.net/

❏ **RealNetworks**
www.prognet.com/

❏ **Voxware**
www.voxware.com/

Multimedia Site Examples

These sites are listed here specifically because they emphasize the use of multimedia products. Expect to see motion and hear sound or to be nagged to get the software that will let you do it. Note, however, that many of the sites listed in other categories also use multimedia.

❏ **Addicted to Noise**
www.addict.com/

❏ **Akimbo Design**
www.akimbodesign.com/

❏ **Alice's Adventures in Wonderland**
http://megabrands.com/alice/indexx.html

❏ **Andy's Garage Sale**
www.andysgarage.com/

❏ **Babylon 5**
www.babylon5.com/cmp/

❏ **Billabong**
www.billabong.com/

❑ **Citizen Kanine**
www.ammg.com/Virtuville/K9/kanine.html

❑ **Clevermedia Shockwave Arcade Games**
clevermedia.com/arcade/

❑ **Colenso**
webnz.com/colenso/

❑ **Colgate**
www.colgate.com/Kids-world/Jungle/

❑ **Diet Coke**
www.dietcoke.com/

❑ **DreamWorks Records**
www.dreamworksrec.com/

❑ **Fox Kids Online**
www.foxkids.com/

❑ **Frog Design**
www.frogdesign.com

❑ **GapKids**
www.gapkids.com/

❑ **Habanero Computing Solutions**
www.habanero.com/

❑ **Halloween Cards**
www.123cards.com/halloween/
animatedcards/index.html

❑ **Homewrecker**
www.homewrecker.com/main.html

❑ **Hot Wheels**
www.hotwheels.com/speedcity/

❑ **IBM Research Demo**
www.research.ibm.com/research/demos/
gmr/index.html

❑ **Lego Tecnic City**
www.lego.com/technic/cybermaster/
cyberscoop.asp

❑ **Nike**
www.Nike.com

❑ **Pandora Interactive Studio**
www.pandora.com.sg/

❑ **Peugot**
www.peugeot206.co.uk/

❑ **Pop Rocket's Shockwave Game Arena**
www.poprocket.com/welcome.html

❑ **Progressive Mobile Electronics**
www.progressivemobile.com/index2.html

❑ **Robot Dancer**
www.multimania.com/goprof/fsdancer.htm

❑ **Rod Stewart**
www.rodstewartlive.com/mxrodhome.html

❑ **Saatchi and Saatchi**
www.saatchi-saatchi.com/

❑ **Spy Watch**
www.bbc.co.uk/education/lookandread/

❑ **The Park**
www.the-park.com/

❑ **Ultra Lounge**
www.ultralounge.com/

❏ **Warner Brothers**
www.warnerbros.com/

❏ **Wet Cement**
www.lasvegassun.com/sun/dossier/events/
cementkid/game.html

Museums

*Actual museums are available in many locales,
but those in distant places are now available—
and beautifully presented—online.*

❏ **7th Museum**
www.Desk.nl/~seventh/

❏ **American Museum of Natural History**
www.amnh.org/

❏ **American Museum of Photography**
www.photographymuseum.com/

❏ **Andy Warhol Museum**
www.warhol.org/

❏ **B & O Railroad Museum**
www.borail.org/

❏ **Bad Fads Museum**
www.adscape.com/badfads/

❏ **Cooper-Hewitt National Design Museum**
www.si.edu/ndm/dfl/

❏ **de Young**
www.thinker.org/index.shtml

❏ **Drop Zone**
www.thedropzone.org/

❑ **Exploratorium**
www.exploratorium.edu/

❑ **Franklin Institute Science Museum**
sln.fi.edu/

❑ **Graphion's Online Type Museum**
www.slip.net/~graphion/museum.html

❑ **Guggenheim Museum**
www.guggenheim.org/

❑ **Guide to Museums and Cultural Resources**
www.lam.mus.ca.us/webmuseums/

❑ **Henry Ford Museum**
hfm.umd.umich.edu/

❑ **Holocaust Museum**
www.mznet.org/chamber/

❑ **Holography Museum**
www.holoworld.com/

❑ **Hudson River Museum**
www.hrm.org/

❑ **Insect Museum**
www.insecta.com/

❑ **Institute and Museum of History of Science**
galileo.imss.firenze.it/

❑ **Isamu Noguchi Museum**
www.noguchi.org/

❑ **Israel Museum**
www.imj.org.il/

❏ **Le Musee de Beaux-Arts**
www.mmfa.qc.ca/

❏ **Metropolitan Museum of Art**
www.metmuseum.org/htmlfile/gallery/
gallery.html

❏ **Murnau Castle Museum**
www.lrz-muenchen.de/~kl921aa/WWW/
index2.html

❏ **Musee Rodin**
www.musee-rodin.fr/

❏ **Museum of Antiques**
www.ncl.ac.uk/~nantiq/

❏ **Museum of Dirt**
www.planet.com/dirtweb/dirt.html

❏ **Museum of Surgical Science**
www.imss.org/

❏ **Museum of Women's History**
www.nmwh.org/

❏ **Museum of Television and Radio**
www.mtr.org/

❏ **Museum of the City of New York**
www.mcny.org/

❏ **National Museum of Australia**
www.nma.gov.au/

❏ **Natural History Museum**
www.nhm.ac.uk/

❏ **Newseum**
www.newseum.org

❏ **Olympic Museum**
www.museum.olympic.org/

❏ **Obsolete Computer Museum**
www.obsoletecomputermuseum.org/

❏ **Peabody Museum of Archaeology and Ethnology**
www.peabody.harvard.edu/

❏ **Philadelphia Museum of Art**
www.philamuseum.org/

❏ **Photo Museum**
www.photographymuseum.com/

❏ **Smithsonian**
www.si.edu/

❏ **Tech Museum of Innovation**
www.thetech.org/

❏ **Tenement Museum**
www.wnet.org/tenement/

❏ **The Acropolis Museum**
www.culture.gr/2/21/211/21101m/
e211am01.html

❏ **The Museum of Costume**
www.museumofcostume.co.uk/

❏ **The Museum of HP Calculators**
www.hpmuseum.org/

❏ **The Museum of Modern Art**
www.moma.org/

❏ **U.S. Holocaust Memorial Museum**
www.ushmm.org/

❑ **Van Gogh Museum**
www.vangoghmuseum.nl/

❑ **Whitney Museum of American Art**
www.whitney.org/

Music

Can we cover all types of music in this short list? We've tried. But if you have an interest that's not mentioned here, a search engine will probably uncover matching sites.

❑ **African Music Encyclopedia**
africanmusic.org/

❑ **American Music Therapy Association**
www.musictherapy.org/

❑ **Artist Underground**
www.aumusic.com/

❑ **Black Countdown**
www.galactica.it/101/black/top40.html

❑ **Classical Insites**
www.classicalinsites.com/

❑ **FenderWorld**
www.fender.com/

❑ **Harmony Music List**
www.sdam.com/harmony/

❑ **Instrument Encyclopedia**
www.si.umich.edu/CHICO/MHN/
enclpdia.html

❑ **International Lyrics Server**
www.lyrics.ch/

❏ **Internet Beatles Album**
www.liv.ac.uk/ipm/beatles

❏ **J. S. Bach Home Page**
www.tile.net/tile/bach/index.html

❏ **Jazz Online**
www.jazzonln.com/

❏ **Knitting Factory**
www.knittingfactory.com/

❏ **MP3**
www.mp3.com/

❏ **MTV Online**
www.mtv.com/

❏ **Music in the Public Domain**
www.pdinfo.com/list.htm

❏ **MusicSearch**
musicsearch.com/

❏ **Music Theory Online**
boethius.music.ucsb.edu/mto/mtohome.html

❏ **My Launch**
www.mylaunch.com/

❏ **Napster**
www.napster.com/

❏ **Piano on the Net**
www.artdsm.com/music.html

❏ **Picklehead Music**
www.picklehead.com/

❏ **Pollstar**
www.addict.com/

❏ **RadioSpy**
www.radiospy.com/

❏ **Ragtime**
www.ragtimers.org/~ragtimers/

❏ **Red Hot Jazz Archive**
www.redhotjazz.com/

❏ **Roadie.net**
www.roadie.net/

❏ **Rock and Roll Hall of Fame**
www.rockhall.com

❏ **Rocktropolis**
www.rocktropolis.com/rt4/

❏ **SonicNet**
www.sonicnet.com

❏ **Strange and Beautiful Music**
www.strangeandbeautiful.com/

❏ **StreetSound**
www.streetsound.com/

❏ **Toonman**
www.toonman.com/start.html

❏ **Ultimate Band List**
ubl.com/ubl.html

❏ **Vibe**
www.vibe.com/

❏ **Wall of Sound**
wallofsound.go.com/index.html

❏ **Webnoize**
www.webnoize.com/

❏ **Young Composers**
www.youngcomposers.com/

Nature

This list is fairly short because most nature-related sites have environmental overtones and have been listed in that category; see also Save the Planet.

❏ **Aldo Leopold Nature Center**
www.naturenet.com/alnc/

❏ **Bear Den**
www.nature-net.com/bears/

❏ **Butterfly Website**
butterflywebsite.com/awards.htm

❏ **Canadian Nature Federation**
www.cnf.ca/

❏ **Connecting with Nature**
www.pacificrim.net/~nature/

❏ **English Nature**
www.english-nature.org.uk/

❏ **Forces of Nature**
library.thinkquest.org/C003603/english/
index.shtml

❏ **GORP Wildlife**
www.gorp.com/gorp/activity/wildlife.htm

❏ **Nature and Awareness School**
www.nature.valleyva.com/

❏ **Nature Journal**
www.nature.com/

❏ **Nature Park Home Page**
www.naturepark.com/

❏ **Nature Photo Gallery**
www.naturephotogallery.com/

❏ **Nature Photo Index**
www.naturepix.com/

❏ **Nature Rangers**
www.naturerangers.com/

❏ **Nature Smart**
www.naturesmart.com/

❏ **Nature's Classroom**
www.naturesclassroom.org/

❏ **Second Nature: Education for Sustainability**
www.2nature.org/

❏ **Species in the Park**
ice.ucdavis.edu/nps/

❏ **The Nature Conservancy of Colorado**
www.tnccolorado.org/

❏ **Wild Wings: Heading North**
north.audubon.org/

News

Breaking news often shows up on the Internet long before it reaches traditional news media. Beyond that, news reaches a new level of convenience on the Internet: You can take what you want from a great variety of sources.

❏ **ABC News**
www.abcnews.com/

❏ **AJR NewsLink**
www.newslink.org/

❏ **BBC**
www.bbc.co.uk/

❏ **Boston Globe**
www.boston.com/globe/

❏ **CBS News**
uttm.com/headline/welcome.html

❏ **Chicago Tribune**
www.chicagotribune.com

❏ **Detroit News Direct**
www.detnews.com

❏ **European Newspapers**
www.nyu.edu/pages/unionlist/

❏ **Fox News**
www.foxnews.com

❏ **InfoJunkie**
www.infojunkie.com/

❏ **Los Angeles Times**
www.latimes.com/

❏ **Morrock News Service**
www.morrock.com/

❏ **MSNBC**
www.msnbc.com/news/default.asp

❏ **Nando Times**
www.nando.net/

❏ **NBC News**
www.nbc.com/

❏ **New Century Network**
www.newcentury.net/

❏ **New York Times**
www.nytimes.com/

❏ **Newsies on the Web**
www.newsies.com/

❏ **Newsroom**
www.auburn.edu/~vestmon/news.html

❏ **NPR Online**
www.npr.org/

❏ **Online NewsHour**
www.pbs.org/newshour

❏ **Point**
www.pbs.org/point/

❏ **Positive Press**
www.positivepress.com/

❏ **Real News Page**
www.rain.org/~openmind/realnews.htm

❏ **Russia Today**
www.russiatoday.com/

❏ **San Francisco Chronicle**
www.sfgate.com/chronicle/index.shtml

❏ **San Francisco Examiner**
www.examiner.com/

❏ **Sun-Sentinel**
www.sun-sentinel

❏ **Touch Today**
www.clickit.com/touch/news/news.htm

❏ **U.S. News**
www.usnews.com/usnews/

❏ **USA Today**
www.usatoday.com

❏ **Washington Post**
www.washingtonpost.com

❏ **Yahoo News Image Gallery**
dailynews.yahoo.com/headlines/g/ts/

Nothing Better to Do

We don't claim that these sites have any specific value. We're talking soap operas and lost socks here. But if you truly have nothing better to do, take a quick look.

❏ **An Entirely Other Day**
www.eod.com/index.html

❏ **Anonymous Messenger**
www.smalltime.com/nowhere/anon/

❏ **April Fools**
www.aprilfools.com

❏ **As the Web Turns**
www.metzger.com/soap/

❏ **Bad Cookie**
www.badcookie.com

❏ **Bizarre Stuff You Can Make in Your Kitchen**
freeweb.pdq.net/headstrong/

❏ **Blank Page**
www.avnet.co.uk/russ-sky/blank.htm

❏ **Boring Institute**
www.boringinstitute.com/

❏ **Bureau of Missing Socks**
www.jagat.com/joel/socks.html

❏ **Cool404**
www.cool404.com

❏ **Dancing Robot**
www.multimania.com/goprof/fsdancer.htm

❏ **Distortions**
www.quirked.com/distortions/

❏ **Click-and-Drag Poetry**
prominence.com/java/poetry/

❏ **Elvis Lives**
wsrv.clas.virginia.edu/~ads5d/elvis.html

❏ **Extra Cripsy**
www.extracrispy.com/

❏ **Famous Insults**
members.aol.com/WordPlays/insultfp.html

❏ **Famous People's Wills**
www.ca-probate.com/wills.htm

❏ **Flying Pigs**
user.icx.net/~midgard/favlinks/

❏ **Futile**
www.futile.com/index2.html

❏ **Gallery of Misused Quotation Marks**
www.juvalamu.com/qmarks

❏ **Hair Police**
www.hairpolice.com/

❏ **IQ Test**
www.iqtest.com/

❏ **Klutz**
www.klutz.com/

❏ **Mister Poll**
www.misterpoll.com/

❏ **Nostradamus Toolkit**
www.ame.com/

❏ **Other People's Problems**
www2.paramount.com/opp/index.html

❏ **Rhyme Generator**
www.pangloss.com/seidel/Poem/

❏ **Rogue Market**
roguemarket.com/

❏ **Rubberband Ball**
www.easttexas.com/pdlg/theball.htm

❑ **Scary Sites of the Net**
people.ce.mediaone.net/bcbeatty/scary.htm

❑ **The Ratings**
www.brunching.com/ratings/

❑ **This Is True**
www.thisistrue.com/

❑ **Urban Legends Archive**
www.urbanlegends.com/

❑ **Voyeur**
voyeur.mckinley.com/cgi-bin/voyeur.cgi

❑ **Weeno**
www.weeno.com/

❑ **Where's George?**
www.wheresgeorge.com/

❑ **Yesterland**
www.mcs.net/~werner/yester.html

Online 'Zines—Internet and Computer

It's a natural: Use a computer forum to write about computers. The magazines here fall into two categories: those that are online versions of printed matter and those that stand on their own on the Internet.

❑ **Alphabetical List of Computer Magazines/E-zines**
www.hitmill.com/internet/magazines.html

❏ **AtoZintheMail.com**
atozinthemail.com/doitforfree-inthe-mail.htm

❏ **Byte**
www.byte.com/

❏ **Computer Bits Online**
www.computerbits.com/

❏ **Computer Connections**
www.computerconnections.com/

❏ **Computer E-Zines!**
www.teachers-connect.net/cc/
99-00/ezines.htm

❏ **Computer News Daily**
nytsyn.com/live/Latest/

❏ **Computer Underground Digest Archives**
www.eff.org/pub/Misc/Publications/CuD/

❏ **ComputerWorld**
www.computerworld.com

❏ **Eclipse Ezine**
www.eff.org/pub/Misc/Publications/CuD/

❏ **Hyperstand**
www.hyperstand.com/

❏ **iBoost Newsletters**
www.iboost.com/info/newsletters.htm

❏ **Interactive Week**
www4.zdnet.com/intweek/

❏ **Internet World**
www.internetworld.com/

❏ **Internet World**
www.internetworld.com/

❏ **Internet.com**
www.internet.com/

❏ **Mac Today**
mactoday.com/

❏ **Macworld**
macworld.zdnet.com/

❏ **MagNet Interactive**
www.magnet-i.com/

❏ **Media Central**
www.mediacentral.com/

❏ **NetSlaves**
www.disobey.com/netslaves

❏ **Netsurfer Digest**
www.netsurf.com/nsd/index.html

❏ **NewsLinx**
www.newslinx.com/

❏ **Next Generation**
www.next-generation.com/

❏ **One by Zero**
www.coolstartups.com/onebyzero

❏ **PC Computing**
www.zdnet.com/pccomp/

❏ **PC Magazine**
www.pcmag.com/

❏ **PC Today**
www.pctoday.com/

❏ **Road Warrior News**
warrior.com/index.html

❏ **Slate**
www.slate.com/

❏ **Smart Computing**
www.smartcomputing.com/Default.asp

❏ **Stating the Obvious**
www.theobvious.com/index.html

❏ **The Net Net**
www.thenetnet.com/

❏ **Web Review**
www.webreview.com/

❏ **WebNovice Online**
www.webnovice.com/

❏ **Windows Magazine**
www.winmag.com/

❏ **Wired News**
www.wired.com/news/

❏ **Yahoo Internet Life**
www.yil.com

Online 'Zines—Varied

Other than information about the Internet itself, perhaps no type of site has grown as quickly as the online magazine. This selection demonstrates the diversity of the offerings.

❑ **Atlantic Monthly**
www.theatlantic.com/coverj.htm

❑ **Bad Golf**
www.badgolfmonthly.com/

❑ **Billboard**
www.billboard-online.com/

❑ **Black World Today**
www.tbwt.com/

❑ **Cheapskate Monthly**
www.cheapsk8.com/

❑ **Communication Arts**
www.commarts.com/

❑ **Cricket Magazine Group**
www.cricketmag.com/home.html

❑ **Daily Muse**
www.cais.net/aschnedr/muse.htm

❑ **DesertUSA**
www.desertusa.com/

❑ **Disgruntled**
www.disgruntled.com/dishome.html

❑ **Farm Journal Today**
www.farmjournal.com/

❑ **Feed**
www.feedmag.com/

❑ **Firehouse**
www.firehouse.com/

❏ **Gadget**
www.gadgetnews.com/

❏ **George**
www.georgemag.com/contents.html

❏ **Go Inside**
goinside.com/

❏ **Halfway To Hell**
members.tripod.com/HalfwayToHell/main.
htm

❏ **Handbook of the Preapocalypse**
www.nmia.com/~dhlr

❏ **Harpoon**
www.harpoonmag.com

❏ **Inquisitor**
www.inquisitor.com/

❏ **Literal Latte**
www.literal-latte.com/

❏ **Mississippi Review**
sushi.st.usm.edu/mrw/

❏ **National Geographic**
www.nationalgeographic.com/

❏ **Officiana Bohemia**
www.bohemialab.com/

❏ **Old Farmer's Almanac**
www.almanac.com

❏ **Oyster Boy Review**
sunsite.unc.edu/ob/index.html

❏ **Page670**
www.users.zetnet.co.uk/mrdaveo/170.htm

❏ **Pain Killer, Inc.**
www.painkiller.org

❏ **Pandora's Box**
ourworld.compuserve.com/homepages/
christatos/bdpgb.htm

❏ **Papermag**
www.papermag.com/

❏ **Paradigm Shift!**
members.aol.com/para93/index.html

❏ **Personal Technology from the Wall Street Journal**
ptech.wsj.com/

❏ **Retro**
www.retroactive.com/

❏ **Roll Call**
www.rollcall.com/

❏ **Rolling Stone**
www.rollingstone.com/

❏ **Salon**
www.salonmagazine.com

❏ **Scientific American**
www.sciam.com/

❏ **Spaceviews**
www.spaceviews.com/

❑ **Straight Dope**
www.straightdope.com/

❑ **Supernation**
www.supernation.com/

❑ **Surfer Mag**
www.surfermag.com

❑ **Technology Review**
www.techreview.com/

❑ **Urban Desires**
www.desires.com/

❑ **Utne Online**
www.utne.com/

❑ **Vapor Trails**
www.vaportrails.com/

❑ **Village Voice**
www.villagevoice.com/

❑ **Whole Pop**
www.wholepop.com/

❑ **X-Project Paranormal Magazine**
www.xproject-paranormal.com

❑ **Y'all**
www.yall.com/

Outdoor Recreation

Stories and resources and advice and places to go — It's all here.

❑ **23 Peaks**
www.23peaks.com/

❑ **ActiveUSA**
www.activeusa.com/

❑ **All Outdoors**
www.alloutdoors.com/

❑ **American Camping Association**
www.acacamps.org/

❑ **America Outdoors**
www.americaoutdoors.com/

❑ **Appalachian Trail**
www.fred.net/kathy/at.html

❑ **Backpacker**
www.thebackpacker.com/

❑ **Big Wall Climbing**
www.primenet.com/~midds/

❑ **Bluemanna**
www.bluemanna.com.au/

❑ **Body Glove**
www.bodyglove.com/

❑ **Camping France**
www.campingfrance.com/

❑ **CampNet America**
www.kiz.com/campnet/html/campnet.htm

❑ **Climbing Magazine**
www.climbing.com/

❏ **Divernet**
www.divernet.com/

❏ **E-Flight**
e-flight.com/e-flight/

❏ **EMS Climbing School**
www.emsclimb.com/

❏ **Fishing.com**
www.fishing.com/

❏ **Fishing Fool's World**
www.webcom.com/~towns/fish/fish.html

❏ **Fishing World**
www.fishingworld.com/Entry.html

❏ **Go Camping America**
www.gocampingamerica.com

❏ **GoSki.com**
www.goski.com/

❏ **Grand Tour**
www.princeton.edu/~oa/oa.html

❏ **Great Outdoor Recreational Page**
www.gorp.com

❏ **Great Outdoors**
greatoutdoors.com/

❏ **Horse Trails**
www.horsetrails.com/

❏ **Mount Kenya Mountain Climbing**
www.kenya-travels.com/kenyasafaris/
mountclimb.htm

❑ **Mountain Bike Resources**
www.mbronline.com/

❑ **Mountain Climbing on Crete**
www.rethymnon.com/Clients/mountain/

❑ **National Caves**
www.cavern.com/

❑ **National Park Service**
www.nps.gov/

❑ **Outdoor Adventure Sports**
www.outdoorsource.com/

❑ **Outdoor Explorer**
www.outdoorexplorer.com/

❑ **Outdoor Resource**
www.outdoorsource.com/

❑ **Park Search**
www.llbean.com/parksearch/

❑ **Parks Around the World**
www.gorp.com/gorp/resource/
US_National_Park/intlpark.htm

❑ **Pilots and Aviation**
www.landings.com/aviation.html

❑ **Quokka**
www.quokka.com/

❑ **Red River Diary**
www.manflood.com/

❑ **Rock and Ice**
www.rockandice.com/

❏ **SkiCentral**
www.skicentral.com/

❏ **TrailWalk**
www.trailwalk.com/

❏ **Volksmarch Index**
www.ava.org/

People Connection

If you want to find someone you know or find out something about someone you don't know, Internet resources outstrip all others.

❏ **411 Locate.com**
www.411locate.com/

❏ **AnyWho**
www.anywho.com/

❏ **Bigfoot**
www.bigfoot.com/

❏ **Child Quest International**
www.childquest.org/

❏ **Directory of High School Reunions**
www.memorysite.com/reunions/

❏ **Find a Grave**
www.findagrave.com/

❏ **Find Me Now**
findmenow.virtualave.net/

❏ **find-people.de**
www.find-people.de/

❏ **GTE SuperPages**
uperpages.gte.net/

❏ **How to Find People's E-mail Addresses**
www.cs.queensu.ca/FAQs/email/finding.html

❏ **Liszt**
www.liszt.com/

❏ **Notable Citizens of Planet Earth**
www.search.com/Single/0,7,200482,00.html

❏ **PeopleFind.com**
www.peoplefind.com/

❏ **Personal Pages Worldwide**
www.utexas.edu/world/personal/index.html

❏ **Real People, Real Stories**
members.aol.com/gmanacsa/realpage.html

❏ **Reunion Hall**
www.xscom.com/reunion/

❏ **ReunionNet**
www.reunited.com/

❏ **Seeker**
www.the-seeker.com/

❏ **Student.com**
www.student.com/feature/ppd/

❏ **Switchboard**
www.switchboard.com/

❑ **Ultimate People Finder**
www.knowx.com/free/peoplefinder.htm

❑ **Webgrrls**
www.webgrrls.com/

❑ **WhoWhere**
www.whowhere.com/

❑ **Yahoo! People Search**
people.yahoo.com/

Performing Arts

Opera, ballet, mime, and other activities that involve performances can be found here.

❑ **American Ballet Theater**
www.abt.org/

❑ **ArtsEdge**
artsedge.kennedy-center.org/

❑ **ArtsLynx**
www.artslynx.org/

❑ **Ballet Dictionary**
www.abt.org/dictionary/

❑ **Bolshoi Theater**
www.bolshoi.ru/eng/frame.html

❑ **Carnegie Hall**
www.carnegiehall.org/

❑ **Coleman Theatre**
www.coleman.miami.ok.us/

❏ **CultureFinder**
www.culturefinder.com/index.htm

❏ **Culturekiosque**
www.culturekiosque.com/

❏ **Cyberdance**
www.thepoint.net/~raw/dance.htm

❏ **International Society for the Performing Arts Foundation**
ispa-online.org/

❏ **John F. Kennedy Center for the Performing Arts**
www.kennedy-center.org/

❏ **Le Centre du Silence**
www.indranet.com/lcds.html

❏ **Opera America**
www.operaam.org/

❏ **Opera Schedule Server**
www.fsz.bme.hu/opera/main.html

❏ **Performing Arts Data Services**
www.pads.ahds.ac.uk/

❏ **Performing Arts Studio**
www.pastudio.com/

❏ **Royal Opera House**
www.royalopera.org/

❏ **Royal Shakespeare Company**
www.rsc.org/uk/

❏ **San Francisco Opera**
www.sfopera.com/

❏ **Stomp**
www.stomponline.com/

❏ **Voice of Dance**
www.voiceofdance.org/Dance/

Photography

Both professional and amateur samples are available for your viewing pleasure and, in some cases, for purchase.

❏ **A Short Course in Digital Photography**
www.shortcourses.com/book01/contents.htm

❏ **American Museum of Photography**
www.photographymuseum.com/

❏ **Art of Pinhole Photography**
www.pinhole.com/

❏ **Black Star**
www.blackstar.com/

❏ **California Museum of Photography**
cmpl.ucr.edu

❏ **Cheese Magazine**
www.cheesemagazine.com/

❏ **Crime Scene and Evidence Photography**
www.crime-scene-investigator.net/
csi-photo.html

❑ **Converge**
idt.net/~robertp/

❑ **Corbis**
www.corbis.com

❑ **Galaxy Photography**
www.galaxyphoto.com/

❑ **Images of Jazz**
www.leonardjazz.com/

❑ **Index Stock**
www.indexstock.com

❑ **Lightning Photography**
www.weather-photography.com/Lightning/

❑ **Lunar Photography**
www.u-net.com/ph/mas/observe/
lunar-p/lunar-p.htm

❑ **Masters of Photography**
masters-of-photography.com/

❑ **Mountain Gallery**
www.cs.berkeley.edu/~qtluong/gallery/

❑ **Mythopoeia**
www.myth.com/

❑ **PhotoDisc**
www.photodisc.com/

❑ **Photography.com**
www.photography.com/

❑ **Stock Solution**
www.tssphoto.com

❏ **StockPhoto**
www.s2f.com/STOCKPHOTO/

❏ **Storm Photos**
www.photolib.noaa.gov/

❏ **The Civil War Photography Center**
www.civilwarphotography.com/

❏ **The Sight3**
thesight.com/

❏ **Times Square Photography Project**
www.timessquarephotos.org/

❏ **Underwater Photography**
weber.u.washington.edu:80/~scotfree

❏ **White House News Photographers
Association**
www.whnpa.org/

❏ **ZoneZero**
www.zonezero.com/

Political Science

*If you are interested in a specific political issue,
be assured that a search engine will locate
many sites on that topic. The sites listed here,
however, are generic and address the overall
political scene.*

❏ **AllPolitics**
AllPolitics.com/

❏ **America Votes**
scriptorium.lib.duke.edu/americavotes/

❑ **Candidates, Campaigns, and Elections**
www.votenet.com/

❑ **Captiol Hill Blue**
www.capitolhillblue.com/index.htm

❑ **Congressional Q & A**
www.c-span.org/questions/

❑ **Digital Democracy**
www.cdt.org/action/

❑ **Do It Yourself Congressional Investigation**
www.crp.org/diykit/

❑ **Election Connection**
www.gspm.org/electcon/

❑ **Election Notes**
www.klipsan.com/elecnews.htm

❑ **Elections Around the World**
www.agora.stm.it/elections/election/home.htm

❑ **Federal Election Commission**
www.fec.gov/

❑ **Gallup Organization**
www.gallup.com/

❑ **In the Public Interest**
www.sfbg.com/nader/

❑ **Jefferson Project**
www.capweb.net/classic/jefferson/

❑ **National Election Studies**
www.umich.edu/~nes/

❏ **National Political Index**
www.politicalindex.com/

❏ **Open Secrets**
www.opensecrets.org/home/index.asp

❏ **Opinion Polls**
www.pollingreport.com/

❏ **Policy.com**
www.policy.com/

❏ **Political Database of the Americas**
www.georgetown.edu/pdba/

❏ **Political Graveyard**
www.potifos.com/tpg/

❏ **Political Site of the Day**
www.aboutpolitics.com/

❏ **Politics1**
www.politics1.com/

❏ **Polling Report**
www.pollingreport.com/

❏ **Public Campaign**
www.publicampaign.org/

❏ **Public Citizen**
www.citizen.org/

❏ **Public Affairs Web**
www.publicaffairsweb.com/

❏ **Roll Call**
www.rollcall.com/

❑ **Soft Money Laundromat**
www.commoncause.org/laundromat/

❑ **The Hill**
www.hillnews.com/

❑ **Third Party Time?**
www.ksg.harvard.edu/case/3pt/

❑ **Web White and Blue**
www.webwhiteblue.org/

❑ **White House Project**
www.thewhitehouseproject.org/index2.html

Reference and Research

A key advantage of the Internet is that you can find information about just about anything. These particular sites specialize in getting some of that information organized and presenting it in a searchable manner.

❑ **10,000 Year Calendar**
calendarhome.com/tyc/

❑ **50 State Capitals**
www.flags.net/

❑ **Acronym Lookup**
www.ucc.ie/cgi-bin/acronym

❑ **Acronyms and Abbreviations**
www.ucc.ie/cgi-bin/acronym

❏ **American Biographies**
www.gms.ocps.k12.fl.us/biopage/bio.html

❏ **Annals of Improbable Research**
www.improb.com/

❏ **Ask Dr. Dictionary**
www.dictionary.com/

❏ **AUTOPEDIA**
autopedia.com/

❏ **Bartlett's Familiar Quotations**
www.cc.columbia.edu/acis/bartleby/bartlett/

❏ **Britannica Online**
www.britannica.com

❏ **CIA World Factbook**
www.odci.gov/cia/publications/factbook/
index.html

❏ **Classical Composer Biographies**
www.cl.cam.ac.uk/users/mn200/music/
composers.html

❏ **Common Errors in English**
www.wsu.edu:8080/~brains/errors/index.
html

❏ **Congressional Biographical Directory**
bioguide.congress.gov/

❏ **Copyright Archive**
copyrightarchive.com

❏ **Encyclopedia of Psychology**
www.psychology.org/

❏ **Flags of All Countries**
www.wave.net/upg/immigration/flags.html

❏ **Funk and Wagnalls Encyclopedia**
www.funkandwagnalls.com/

❏ **Glass Encyclopedia**
www.encyclopedia.netnz.com/

❏ **go.grolier.com**
gme.grolier.com/

❏ **Guinness Book of Records**
www.guinnessrecords.com/

❏ **Harper's Index**
www.harpers.org/harpers-index/
harpers-index.html

❏ **IPL Reference Center**
www.ipl.org/ref/

❏ **Library of Congress Reading Room**
icweb.loc.gov/global/ncp/ncp.html

❏ **Library Spot**
www.libraryspot.com/

❏ **Measurement Converter**
www.mplik.ru:8081/~sg/transl/

❏ **Musical Instrument Encyclopedia**
www.lehigh.edu/zoellner/encyclopedia.
html

❏ **National Archives**
www.nara.gov/

❏ **Office of Population Research**
opr.princeton.edu/

❑ **Online Intelligence Project**
www.icg.org/intelweb/index.html

❑ **Plumb Design's Thesaurus**
www.plumbdesign.com/thesaurus

❑ **Police Ten Codes**
www.jaxnet.com/~habedd/10codes.html

❑ **Pop Clocks**
www.census.gov/main/www/popclock.html

❑ **Ready Reference Collection**
www.ipl.org/ref/RR/

❑ **Researchpaper.com**
www.researchpaper.com/index.html

❑ **Roget's Thesaurus**
www.thesaurus.com/

❑ **TechEncyclopedia**
www.techweb.com/encyclopedia/

❑ **The Catholic Encyclopedia**
www.newadvent.org/cathen/

❑ **The Virtual Reference Desk**
thorplus.lib.purdue.edu/reference/

❑ **Thomas: Legislative Information**
thomas.loc.gov

❑ **United States Code**
law.house.gov/usc.htm

❑ **Vietnamese Singers' Biographies**
www.vietscape.com/music/singers/

❑ **Virtual Reference Desk**
thorplus.lib.purdue.edu/reference/

❑ **Women's Biographies**
www.distinguishedwomen.com/

❑ **World Flags**
www.flags.net/

❑ **World Time**
www.worldtime.com/

❑ **Yellow Pages USA**
www.bigyellow.com/

Resume Services

Most of these folks will post your Web page resume on their site, sometimes free but usually for a fee. Some also offer advice on making resumes. Others offer resume services as just one service of many.

❑ **#1 Resume Writing Services**
www.free-resume-tips.com/

❑ **123-jobs.com**
www.123-jobs.com/

❑ **1st Impressions Resumes**
www.1st-imp.com/

❑ **A+ Online Resumes**
www.ol-resume.com/

❑ **AAAA-Job Resume Services**
www.aaaa-job.com/

❑ **Aicron Resume Services**
www.aicron.com/

❑ **Career Shop**
www.careershop.com/

❑ **Career Site**
www.careersite.com/

❑ **Global Edge Recruiting**
www.globaledgerecruiting.com/services.asp

❑ **Guaranteed Resume**
www.gresumes.com/

❑ **Job Direct**
www.jobdirect.com/

❑ **QuestCareer.com**
www.questcareer.com/

❑ **Quicksilver Online Services**
www.qosi.net/careers_resume.htm

❑ **Resume Design**
www.ssd.sscc.ru/misc/Resume

❑ **Resume Innovations**
www.resume-innovations.com/

❑ **Resume Publishing Company**
www.sni.net/cha/trpc.htm

❑ **Resume Store**
www.resumestore.com/main.html

❑ **Resume World**
www.resunet.com/rw/

❏ **Resume Writing by Advantage**
www.advantage-resume.com/

❏ **Resumes on the Web**
www.resweb.com/

❏ **Technical Resume Writing Tips**
www.taos.com/resumetips.html

❏ **Tripod's Resume Builder**
www.tripod.com/explore/jobs_career/resume/

❏ **Virtual Resume**
www.virtualresume.com/

❏ **Wordbusters Resume and Writing Services**
www.wbresumes.com/

Robotics

Most of these sites reflect current robotics developments in university or government labs. But some are commercial or personal sites.

❏ **Basic BEAM Robotics**
members.xoom.com/robots/index.htm

❏ **BEAM Robotics**
nis-www.lanl.gov/robot/

❏ **Berkeley Robotics Lab**
robotics.eecs.berkeley.edu/

❏ **Cambridge Speech Vision and Robotics**
svr-www.eng.cam.ac.uk/

❏ **ETHZ Institute of Robotics**
www.ifr.mavt.ethz.ch/

❑ **Harvard Robotics Laboratory**
hrl.harvard.edu/

❑ **Internet Robotics Sources**
www.cs.indiana.edu/robotics/world.html

❑ **Lab for Perceptual Robotics**
www-robotics.cs.umass.edu/lpr.html

❑ **Laboratory for Perceptual Robotics**
piglet.cs.umass.edu:4321/lpr.html

❑ **Laboratory Robotics Interest Group**
lab-robotics.org/

❑ **Mobile Robot Laboratory**
www.cc.gatech.edu/aimosaic/
robot-lab/MRLHome.html

❑ **NASA Space Telerobotics**
ranier.oact.hq.nasa.gov/telerobotics.html

❑ **RoboShopper**
www.roboshopper.com/

❑ **Robot Home Page**
www.areacom.it/html/arte_cultura/
warworld/ROBOT.HTM

❑ **Robot Wars**
ranier.hq.nasa.fob/telerobotics_page/
coolrobots.html

❑ **Robotics FAQs**
www.frc.ri.cmu.edu/robotics-faq/

❑ **Robotics Research**
www.cs.man.ac.uk/robotics/

❑ **Robotics Resources**
www.eg.bucknell.edu/~robotics/res_frame.
html

❑ **Stanford Robotics Laboratory**
robotics.stanford.edu/

❑ **U.S. Robotics**
www.usr.com/index.asp

Save the People

If you want to help, or want to be helped, these sites offer plenty of information to get you started.

❑ **54 Ways You Can Help the Homeless**
ecosys.drdr.virginia.edu/ways/54.html

❑ **Amnesty International**
www.amnesty.org/

❑ **Charitable Choices**
www.charitablechoices.org/

❑ **CharityNet**
www.idealist.org/

❑ **Children's Hunger Relief Fund**
www.chrf.org/

❑ **Disaster Relief**
www.disasterrelief.org/

❑ **Habitat for Humanity**
www.habitat.org/

❑ **Homeless People's Network**
aspin.asu.edu/hpn/

❑ **HungerWeb**
www.brown.edu/Departments/World_
Hunger_Program/

❑ **I Have a Dream Foundation**
www.ihad.org/

❑ **Idealist**
www.idealist.org/

❑ **InterAction**
www.interaction.org/

❑ **Internet Nonprofit Center**
www.nonprofits.org/

❑ **National Coalition for the Homeless**
www2.ari.net/home/nch/

❑ **Peace Corps**
www.peacecorps.gov/home.html

❑ **Salvation Army**
www.webnet.com.au/clients/salvos/

❑ **Second Harvest**
www.secondharvest.org/

❑ **The Hunger Project**
www.thp.org/

❑ **UNICEF**
www.unicef.org/

❏ **U.S. Committee for Refugees**
www.refugees.org/

Save the Planet

As you can see, many people are already involved in organizations to help the environment. You can check out what they are doing, perhaps take some of their tips for everyday living, or even join them.

❏ **American Forests**
www.amfor.org/

❏ **Arbor Day**
www.arborday.com/

❏ **Bagheera**
www.bagheera.com/

❏ **Center for Nuclear and Toxic Waste Management**
ist-socrates.berkeley.edu:4050/nuc.html

❏ **Climate Action Network**
www.climatenetwork.org/

❏ **Compost Resource Page**
www.oldgrowth.org/compost/

❏ **Conservation International**
www.conservation.org/

❏ **Corporate Watch**
www.corpwatch.org/

❏ **Dolphins: Oracles of the Sea**
library.advanced.org/17963/

❑ **Eagle Page**
www.sky.net/~emily/eagle.html

❑ **Earth Share**
www.earthshare.org/

❑ **EnviroLink**
www.envirolink.org/

❑ **Environmental Legislation**
www.nrdc.org/nrdc/field/state.html

❑ **Environmental Stresses and Tree Health**
www.ianr.unl.edu/pubs/forestry/G1036.htm

❑ **Environmental Yellow Pages**
www.enviroyellowpages.com/

❑ **EPA Global Warming Site**
www.epa.gov/globalwarming/

❑ **Forests Forever**
www.forestsforever.org/

❑ **Friends of the Earth**
www.foe.co.uk/foei/worldmap.html

❑ **Friends of the Environment**
www.fef.ca/

❑ **Garbage**
www.learner.org/exhibits/garbage/intro.html

❑ **Global Eco-Village**
www.gaia.org/

❑ **Global Warming International Center**
www.globalwarming.net/

❑ **GreenMoney Online Guide**
www.greenmoney.com/

❑ **Greenpeace**
www.greenpeaceusa.org/

❑ **InterActivism**
www.interactivism.com/

❑ **International Rivers Network**
www.irn.org/

❑ **Living Africa**
hyperion.advanced.org/16645/contents.html

❑ **Native Environmentalism**
www.indians.org/library/nate.html

❑ **Nature Conservancy**
www.tnc.org/

❑ **Planet Ark**
www.planet.ark.com.au/

❑ **Rainforest Action Network**
www.ran.org/ran/

❑ **Recycler's World**
www.recycle.net/recycle/index.html

❑ **Save Beaches**
beaches.hartford.edu/

❑ **Sea Turtle Survival**
www.cccturtle.org/

❑ **Search Your Watershed**
www.epa.gov/surf2/surf98/wimdw.html

❑ **Seaweb**
www.seaweb.org/

❑ **Sierra Club**
www.sierraclub.org/

❑ **Silicon Valley Joint Venture**
www.jointventure.org/

❑ **Solstice**
solstice.crest.org/index.shtml

❑ **Turtle Trax**
www.turtles.org/

❑ **Whole Earth**
www.wholeearthmag.com/

❑ **Wild Things**
www.cris.com/~cheeta/

❑ **Wilderness Society**
wilderness.org/

❑ **Wildlife Web**
www.selu.com/~bio/sildlife/

❑ **Wolf's Den**
www.wolfsden.org/

❑ **World Conservation**
www.wcmc.org.uk/

❑ **World Map for Whale Watchers**
www.physics.helsinki.fi/whale/world.html

❑ **World Wildlife Federation**
www.wwf.org/

Science

Scientific interests have been presented on the Internet from the beginning. If you are involved in science in any way, whether you are just taking a class or you make your living in the scientific community or simply have a keen curiosity, your particular interest is probably represented in several sites on the Internet. See also Mathematics.

❏ **Amusement Park Physics**
www.learner.org/exhibits/parkphysics/

❏ **Astronomy.com**
www.kalmbach.com/astro/astronomy.html

❏ **Bad Science Page**
www.ems.psu.edu/~fraser/BadScience.html

❏ **BillNye.com**
nyelabs.kcts.org/

❏ **BioTech**
biotech.chem.indiana.edu/

❏ **Biographies of Scientists**
www.blupete.com/Literature/Biographies/
Science/Scients.htm

❏ **Biology Project**
www.biology.arizona.edu/

❏ **BioTech**
biotech.iocmb.utexas.edu/

❏ **Botanical Glossaries**
sln.fi.edu/biosci/heart.html

❏ **ChemFinder**
chemfinder.camsoft.com/

❏ **Community of Science**
www.cos.com/

❏ **Cool Science Images**
whyfiles.news.wisc.edu/coolimages/

❏ **Dinosauria Online**
www.dinosauria.com/

❏ **Evolutionary Ecology Research**
www.evolutionary-ecology.com/

❏ **The Exploratorium's Ten Cool Sites**
www.exploratorium.edu/learning_studio/
sciencesites.html

❏ **Explore Science**
www.explorescience.com/

❏ **FIRST**
www.usfirst.org/

❏ **FlyBase**
flybase.bio.indiana.edu:82/

❏ **Galileo's Notes on Motion**
www.imss.fi.it/ms72/

❏ **General Chemistry**
chemfinder.camsoft.com/

❏ **History of Science and Technology**
www.asap.unimelb.edu.au/hstm/
hstm_ove.htm

❏ **How Things Work**
landau1.phys.virginia.edu/Education/
Teaching/HowthingsWork/home.html

❏ **Human Anatomy Online**
www.innerbody.com/

❏ **Human Brain**
uta.marymt.edu/~psychol/brain.html

❏ **National Optical Astronomy Observatory**
www.noao.edu/

❏ **Nobel Foundation**
www.nobel.se/

❏ **Ozone Hole Tour**
www.atm.ch.cam.ac.uk/tour/

❏ **Physics FAQ**
math.ucr.edu/home/baez/physics/faq.html

❏ **Profiles in Science**
www.profiles.nlm.nih.gov/

❏ **Quantum Computation**
www.qubit.org/

❏ **Science à GoGo**
www.scienceagogo.com/

❏ **Science Daily**
www.sciencedaily.com/

❏ **Science in the Public Interest**
www.cspinet.org/

❏ **Science Odyssey**
www.pbs.org/wgbh/aso/

❏ **Scientific American**
www.sciam.com/

❏ **Split-Cycle Technology**
www.ozemail.aust.com/~splitcyc/

❏ **The Heart**
sln.fi.edu/biosci/heart.html

❏ **The Why Files**
whyfiles.news.wisc.edu/

❏ **Transistor Science**
www.pbs.org/transistor/

❏ **Virtual Frog Dissection Kit**
george.lbl.gov/ITG.hm.pg.docs/dissect/info.
html

❏ **Visible Human Viewer**
www.npac.syr.edu/projects/vishuman/
VisibleHuman.html

❏ **Visible Human**
www.nlm.nih.gov/research/visible/visible_
human.html

❏ **Volcano World**
volcano.und.nodak.edu/vw.html

Shopping—Books

If you want a particular book that is old, rare, or a bestseller, it's on the Internet. If you just want to browse, the choices are wonderfully endless.

❏ **Alternative Books Superstore**
web-star.com/alternative/books.html

❏ **Amazon Books**
www.amazon.com

❏ **AnyBook International**
www.anybook.com/

❏ **Bargain Book Warehouse**
www.1bookstreet.com/1bargainbookstreet/
Bargain_Home.asp

❏ **Barnes and Noble**
www.barnesandnoble.com/

❏ **Book Collectors Bookstore**
www.abcbooks.com/

❏ **Book Passage**
www.bookpassage.com/

❏ **Bookpool Technical Books**
www.bookpool.com/

❏ **Books.com**
www.books.com

❏ **Borders**
www.borders.com/

❏ **Clean Well-lighted Place for Books**
www.bookstore.com/

❏ **Computer and Internet Books**
home.earthlink.net/~jlutgen/cirob.html

❏ **Fatbrain**
www.clbooks.com/

❏ **Libros en Espanol**
www.sbdbooks.com/

❏ **Midnight Special Bookstore**
www2.msbooks.com/msbooks/homepage.
html

❏ **Powell's Books: Used, New, and Out of Print**
www.powells.com

❏ **Serendipity Books**
www.serendipitybooks.com/

❏ **Varsity Books**
www.varsitybooks.com/

❏ **Vintage Bookstore**
www.vintagelibrary.com/index.cfm

❏ **Virtual Moe's**
moesbooks.com/

❏ **Wantagh Rare Book Company**
www.zelacom.com/~wantagh/

Shopping—Catalogs

Order from the catalog or order from the Internet.

❏ **Art.com**
art.com/

❏ **Bloomingdales**
www.bloomingdales.com/

❏ **Books on Tape**
www.booksontape.com/

❏ **CatalogLink**
cataloglink.com/cl/

❏ **Disney Store**
disney.go.com/Shopping/

❏ **Eastbay**
www.eastbay.com/

❏ **Eddie Bauer**
www.ebauer.com/

❏ **Harry and David**
www.harryanddavid.com/

❏ **J Crew**
jcrew.com/

❏ **Jackson and Perkins**
www.jacksonandperkins.com/

❏ **JCPenney**
www.jcpenney.com/shopping

❏ **L.L. Bean**
www.llbean.com/

❏ **Lands' End**
www.landsend.com/

❏ **Neiman Marcus**
www.neimanmarcus.com/

❏ **Popcorn Factory**
www.thepopcornfactory.com/

❑ **REI**
www.rei.com/

❑ **Spiegel**
www.spiegel.com/spiegel

❑ **Talbots**
www.talbots.com/

❑ **The Company Store**
www.thecompanystore.com/

❑ **The Nature Company**
www.natureco.com/

❑ **Watkins Product Catalog**
futuregate.com/watkins_catalog/index.html

Shopping—Classifieds

*These Internet ads resemble the classifieds ads
in newspapers. All sites here are easy to search.*

❑ **#1 Classifieds**
www.boconline.com/1Classifieds/1fieds.htm

❑ **4* Classifieds**
www.4starads.com/classifieds/

❑ **AdQuest**
www.adquest3d.com/

❑ **AmericaNet.Com**
www.americanet.com/Classified/

❑ **American Internet Classifieds**
www.bestads.com/

❑ **Buy and Sell**
www.buy-and-sell.com/

❏ **Classified Display**
www.classified-display.com/

❏ **Classified Flea Market**
www.cfm.com/

❏ **ClassiFIND**
www.classifind.com/

❏ **Classify It**
www.classify-it.com/

❏ **Emarket Trading Post**
www.emrkt.com/trading_post/

❏ **Epage Internet Classifieds**
www.ep.com/

❏ **Free Classified Ads**
www.freeclassifiedads.com/

❏ **LookSmart Classifieds**
www.classifieds2000.com/
cgi-cls/display.exe?looksmart+class

❏ **The Find**
www.thefind.com/default_tf.asp

❏ **Trader Online Classified Ads**
www.traderonline.com/

Shopping—Computer Hardware, Software, and Stuff

Serious computerphiles can spend many hours sorting out the wares offered by these sites.

❏ Baber's Global Computer Directory
www.baber.com/

❏ Best Buy
www.bestbuy.com

❏ Beyond.com
www.beyond.com/

❏ Black Box
www.blackbox.com/

❏ Build Your Own PC
www.verinet.com/pc/

❏ Buy Direct
www.buydirect.com/?st.snap.dir

❏ Compubooks
www.compubooks.com/

❏ CompUSA Online
www.compusa.com

❏ Computer Craft
www.ccraft.net

❏ Computer Discount Warehouse
www.cdw.com/

❏ Computer Quick
www.cqk.com/

❏ Computer Shopper
www5.zdnet.com/cshopper

❏ Cybermedia
www.cybermedia.com/

❏ **Download.com**
www.download.com/

❏ **Egghead Software**
www.egghead.com/

❏ **E-Town**
www.e-town.com/

❏ **Exploria**
www.exploria.com

❏ **It's Time**
www2.viaweb.com/rks/itstim.html

❏ **NECX Direct**
www.necx.com/

❏ **Online Used Computer Swap**
www.creativelement.com/swap/

❏ **PC Magazine Software**
www.zdnet.com/pcmag/pclabs/software/
software.htm

❏ **PC Shopping Planet**
www.shoppingplanet.com/

❏ **Price Watch**
www.pricewatch.com/

❏ **Screen Savers Bonanza**
www.bonanzas.com/ssavers/index.html

❏ **Second Nature Software**
www.secondnature.com/

❏ **Softchoice**
www.softchoice.com/

❏ **System Optimization**
www.sysopt.com/

❏ **TechShopper**
www.techweb.com/shopper/

❏ **TechWeb**
www.techweb.com/

❏ **Tom's Hardware Guide**
www.sysdoc.pair.com/

❏ **Zing**
www.aing.com

Shopping—General

Popular Internet shopping sites have been arbitrarily divided here into various categories. The "general" sites listed here tend to offer a variety of products or shopping-related services.

❏ **Amazon.com**
www.amazon.com/

❏ **As Seen on TV**
www.asontv.com/

❏ **At Your Office**
www.atyouroffice.com/

❏ **Autobytel.com**
www.autobytel.com/

❏ **BestBuy.com**
www.bestbuy.com/

❑ **Beyond Average Gear**
www.bagear.com/

❑ **Birdwatching Things to Buy**
www.birding.about.com/cs/thingstobuy/

❑ **Bluefly**
www.bluefly.com/

❑ **Buccaneer Trading Company**
www.buccaneer.net/

❑ **Bugle Boy**
www.bugleboy.com/

❑ **Bushel of Baskets**
www.abushelofbaskets.com/

❑ **Buy.com**
www.buy.com/

❑ **CDnow**
www.cdnow.com

❑ **CD Universe**
www.cduniverse.com

❑ **Cigars at Discount**
www.usabuydirect.com/

❑ **CompareNet**
www.compare.net/

❑ **Cool Savings**
www.coolsavings.com

❑ **Corral West Ranchwear**
www.corralwest.com/

❏ **CyberShop**
www.cybershop.com/

❏ **Designer Deals**
www.designerdeals.com

❏ **Discount Games**
www.discountgames.com/

❏ **Fashion Planet**
www.fashion-planet.com

❏ **Filene's Basement**
www.filenesbasement.com/

❏ **First Outlet!**
www.isn.com/

❏ **First Sightings**
www.firstsightings.com/

❏ **Gap**
www.gap.com/onlinestore/gap

❏ **Gift Tree**
www.gifttree.com/

❏ **Hanes.com**
www.hanes.com/wheretobuy.html

❏ **Hewlett-Packard Store**
www.hp.com/Redirect/gw/useng_welcome/
store/=/country/us/eng/hp_store.htm

❏ **Hunting Net**
www.hunting.net/shopping/

❏ **IQVC**
www.iqvc.com

❑ **I-Stores**
www.i-stores.com/

❑ **LetsBuyIt.com**
www.letsbuyit.com/

❑ **MelaNet**
www.melanet.com/

❑ **Music Boulevard**
www.musicblvd.com/

❑ **MySimon**
www.mysimon.com/

❑ **Pacific Trekking**
pacifictrekking.com/

❑ **Patagonia**
www.patagonia.com/

❑ **Peapod**
www.peapod.com/

❑ **Quick Coupons**
www.qpons.com/

❑ **ReviewBooth**
www.reviewbooth.com/

❑ **Roxy**
www.roxy.com/

❑ **Sharper Image**
www.sharperimage.com/

❑ **Shopping Central**
www.ivillage.com/shopping/

❑ **Surplus/Closeout finder**
www.infomart.net/surplus

❑ **TechShopper**
www.techweb.com/shopper/softwarestore

❑ **The Weather Channel's eCompanyStore**
shop.ecompanystore.com/weather/

❑ **Ticketmaster USA**
www.ticketmaster.com/

❑ **Tower Records**
www.tower.records

❑ **Toys 'R' Us**
www.toysrus.com/

❑ **Urbanwhere**
www.urbanwhere.com/

❑ **ValuPage**
www.valupage.com/

❑ **Wellspring Media**
www.wellmedia.com/

Shopping—Mall

Each site on this list is a collection of online stores; that is, it's the same idea as a bricks and mortar mall.

❑ **Access Market Square**
www.amsquare.com/

❑ **Awesome Mall**
malls.com/awesome

❏ **Big Planet**
www.bpstore.com/index.html

❏ **Biggest Mall**
www.biggestmall.com/

❏ **Choice Mall**
mall.choicemall.com/

❏ **Coolshopping**
www.coolshopping.com/

❏ **Cowboy Mall**
www.cowboymall.com/

❏ **Downtown Anywhere**
www.awa.com/index.html

❏ **Duluth Mall**
www.duluthemall.com/

❏ **EcoMall**
www.ecomall.com/

❏ **Empire Mall**
empiremall.com/

❏ **Globalscape Mall**
www.sigmaduke.com/business/

❏ **Great Alaskan Mall**
alaskan.com/

❏ **Hall of Malls**
www.nsns.com/MouseTracks/hall/
general.html

❏ **iMall**
www.imall.com/

❏ **Mall of Cyberspace**
www.zmall.com/

❏ **Mallpark**
www.mallpark.com/

❏ **NeedleArts Mall**
www.needlearts.com/shop_index.html

❏ **Pennsylvania Dutch Marketplace**
www.padutch.com/Welcome.html

❏ **Sell 'Em**
www.sellem.com

❏ **ShopNow**
www.shopnow.com/

❏ **SkyMall**
www.skymall.com/

❏ **Student Mall**
studentcenter.infomall.org/ourmall.html

❏ **Texas Hill Country Mall**
www.texashillcountrymall.com/

❏ **Tropical Mall**
www.naples-fl.com/

❏ **Truly Texan**
www.trulytexan.com/

❏ **Wild West Cybermall**
www.cache.net/westmall/

❏ **World Wide Mall**
www.olworld.com/olworld/mall/mall_us/
dir.html

❏ **WorldShop**
www.worldshop.com/

Shopping—Specialty

The sites in this list offer some specific product or product line—or are just cute little "shops."

❏ **1001 Herbs**
www.1001herbs.com/

❏ **1-800-Batteries**
www.1800batteries.com/home.htm

❏ **1-800-Flowers**
www.1800flowers.com

❏ **Aardvark Pet**
www.aardvarkpet.com/

❏ **All About First Names**
www.personalizedgiftshop.com/

❏ **American Quilts**
www.americanquilts.com/

❏ **American Science and Surplus**
www.sciplus.com/

❏ **Anything Left-handed**
members.aol.com/alhleft/

❏ **Archie McPhee**
www.mcphee.com/

❏ **Aspen Trading Post**
www.aspentradingpost.com/

❏ **Australian Wool Gallery**
www.exton.com/awg/

❏ **Azazz**
www.azazz.com/

❏ **BabyCenter Shopping**
www.babycenter.com/shopping/

❏ **Bird Houses**
www.carpenterslace.com/

❏ **Bliss Spa**
www.blissspa.com/

❏ **Brits Abroad**
www.britsabroad.co.uk/

❏ **Candy Direct**
www.candydirect.com/

❏ **Candlexpress**
www.candlexpress.com/

❏ **Charm Cheese**
www.craftassoc.com/charmcm.html

❏ **Civil War Outpost**
www.civilwaroutpost.com/

❏ **Clown Shoes**
www.jollywalkers.com/

❏ **College Depot**
collegedepot.com/

❏ **DaFridge Magnets**
www.dafridge.com/

❑ **Designer Stencils**
www.designerstencils.com/

❑ **Down to Earth**
www.downtoearth.com/

❑ **Fabric8**
www.fabric8.com/

❑ **Farmacopia**
www.candydirect.com/

❑ **Faucet Factory**
www.faucetfactory.com/

❑ **Fogdog Sports**
www.fogdog.com/

❑ **Gargoyle Statuary**
www.gargoylestatuary.com/

❑ **Hammocks**
www.hameck.com/

❑ **Hollywood Posters**
www.hollywoodsouvenirs.com/pms.html

❑ **Hot Hot Hot**
www.hothothot.com

❑ **Internet Antique Shop**
www.tias.com/

❑ **Internet Auction List**
www.usaweb.com/auction.html

❑ **Internet Bookshop**
www.bookshop.co.uk/

❏ **Intima Watches**
www.intima.com/

❏ **Jam, Jelly, and More**
www.vipimage.com/

❏ **Joy of Socks**
www.joyofsocks.com/

❏ **Justballs**
www.justballs.com/

❏ **Kennedy Space Center Shop**
www.thespaceshop.com/

❏ **Mexican Pottery**
www.awa.com/tp/

❏ **Moon Spirit Gallery**
www.moonchild.com/moonspirit/

❏ **Mother Nature's General Store**
www.mothernature.com/

❏ **Mountain Zone**
www.mountainzone.com/

❏ **Mrs. Fields Cookies**
www.mrsfields.com/

❏ **Navajo Rugs**
navajorugs.spma.org/

❏ **Perfect Present Picker**
presentpicker.com/

❏ **Prima Sports**
www.prima.com/

❑ **Red Rocket**
www.redrocket.com/

❑ **Reel**
www.reel.com

❑ **Relax the Back Store**
www.relaxtheback.com/

❑ **Revo**
www.revo.com

❑ **Rolling Pin Kitchen Emporium**
www.rollingpin.com/

❑ **Rubber Stamp Queen**
www.dol.com/queen/

❑ **Shaker Furniture**
ncnet.com/ncnw/gall-shr.html

❑ **Shoes on the Net**
www.shoesonthenet.com/

❑ **Shop Titanic**
maritimeheritage.com/

❑ **Snookie's Cookies**
www.snookies.com/

❑ **Southpaw Enterprises**
www.southpaw.bc.ca/

❑ **Sovietski Collection**
www.sovietski.com/

❑ **Specialty Linens**
www.specialty-linens.com/

❏ **Submarine Memorabilia**
www.subshipstore.com/

❏ **Sunglass Source**
www.eyeglassplace.com/sunglasses/

❏ **Swiss Army Brands**
www.swissarmy.com

❏ **Texas Branding Company**
www.cowboys.com/texasbrandingironco/

❏ **Time by Design**
timebydesign.com/

❏ **Unclaimed Baggage**
www.unclaimedbaggage.com/

❏ **Violet**
www.violet.com/

❏ **Vitamin Shoppe**
www.vitaminshoppe.com/

❏ **Walkabout Travel Gear**
www.walkabouttravelgear.com/

❏ **Way Out West**
www.wayoutwest.com/

❏ **Wig Outlet**
www.wigs.com/

❏ **Wind-up Toys**
www.winduptoyco.com/

Sounds

Some of these sites have serious information about adding sound to an Internet site. Some, like the Police Scanner, are merely odd uses of sound. But most are examples of how sound can add an extra dimension to a site.

❏ **4AD**
www.4ad.com/

❏ **Jesus Loves You**
www.geocities.com/SiliconValley/Pines/6030/

❏ **Audible**
www.audible.com/

❏ **Ballparks**
www.ballparks.com/

❏ **Bird Sounds**
www.naturesongs.com/birds.html

❏ **Broadcast.com**
www.audionet.com/

❏ **Capitol Steps**
www.capsteps.com/

❏ **Cartoon Sounds**
www.cartoonsounds.com/

❏ **Classical MIDI Archives**
www.prs.net/midi.html

❏ **CowPokin' Fun**
netnow.micron.net/~clj/index.htm

❏ **Daily Feed**
www.dailyfeed.com/

❏ **Daily WAV**
www.dailywav.com/

❏ **Fantasy Jazz**
www.fantasyjazz.com

❏ **FindSounds.com**
findsounds.com/

❏ **FUNNY SOUNDS**
www.funny-sounds.com/

❏ **Historical Speeches**
www.webcorp.com/sounds/index.htm

❏ **JFK Tapes**
www.c-span.org/ram/jfk/jfk012699_04.ram

❏ **Live Concerts**
www.liveconcerts.com

❏ **Live-Online**
www.live-online.com/

❏ **Movies Sounds**
www.moviesounds.com/

❏ **One Stop Jazz**
www.mindspring.com/~kvansant/

❏ **One-on-One Sports**
www.1on1sports.com/

❏ **PoliceScanner.com**
www.policescanner.com/

❏ **RealGuide**
realguide.real.com/

❏ **Site with Audio Clips**
www.geek-girl.com/audioclips.html

❏ **Sites & Sounds**
www.sitesandsounds.com/

❏ **Soundbites**
www.soundbites.com/

❏ **Sounds of Oceania**
www.oceania.org/sounds/

❏ **Sounds Online**
www.soundsonline.com/

❏ **Spinner**
www.spinner.com/

❏ **Standard MIDI files**
www.aitech.ac.jp/~ckelly/SMF.html

❏ **Subaudio**
www.subaudio.net/

❏ **The Library of Natural Sounds**
birds.cornell.edu/LNS/

❏ **The Moonlit Road**
www.themoonlitroad.com/

❏ **The Sound**
www.thesound.com/

❏ **This American Life**
www.thislife.org/

Social Sciences

See also *Economics, History, and Political Science.*

❏ **Ancient World Web**
www.julen.net/aw/

❏ **Anthropology Biographies**
www.anthro.mankato.msus.edu/bio/

❏ **Anthropology Resources on the Internet**
home.worldnet.fr/clist/Anthro/

❏ **Archeology on the Net**
www.serve.com/archaeology/main.html

❏ **Best Practices Database**
www.bestpractices.org/

❏ **Center for Survey Research**
www.fhsu.edu/htmlpages/services/survey/
index.html

❏ **Country Studies: Area Handbook Series**
lcweb2.loc.gov/frd/cs/cshome.html

❏ **Demographics**
www.cnie.org/pop/population.htm

❏ **Indigenous Peoples' Information**
www.halcyon.com/FWDP/

❏ **National Sprawl News Index**
www.interaxs.net/pub/mikemonett/natl.htm

❏ **Psychology with Style**
www.uwsp.edu/acad/psych/apa4b.htm

❑ **Psychology.net**
www.psychology.net/

❑ **Public Opinion Database**
www.ciesin.org/datasets/irss/irss.html

❑ **Race and Ethnic Studies Institute**
resi.tamu.edu/index.html

❑ **Research Resources for the Social Sciences**
www.socsciresearch.com/

❑ **Shaping Our Communities: The Impact of Information Technology**
www.internetcenter.state.mn.us/
Itn-open.htm

❑ **Social Psychology Network**
www.wesleya.edu/spn/

❑ **Social Science Data Archives**
osiris.colorado.edu/SOC/RES/data.html

❑ **Social Statistics Briefing Room**
www.whitehouse.gov/fsbr/ssbr.html

❑ **Uncommonly Difficult IQ Tests**
www.eskimo.com/~miyaguch/hoeflin.html

❑ **Web of Culture**
www.webofculture.com/

Space

Most of these sites, as you might expect, have their origins in NASA. All are informative, and many are breathtaking.

❏ **Ask an Astronaut**
www.nss.org/askastro/

❏ **Astronaut Connection**
nauts.com/

❏ **Cassini: Voyage to Saturn**
www.jpl.nasa.gov/cassini/

❏ **Center for Mars Exploration**
cmex-www.arc.nasa.gov/

❏ **Deep Cold**
www.deepcold.com/

❏ **Earth Images from Space**
code935.gsfc.nasa.gov/Tutorial/TofC/
Coverpage.html

❏ **Earthshots**
edcwww.cr.usgs.gov/Earthshots/

❏ **Hubble Space Telescope**
quest.arc.nasa.gov/interactive/hst.html/

❏ **Mars Society**
www.marssociety.org/

❏ **Messier Catalog**
www.seds.org/messier/

❏ **NASA Human Spaceflight**
station.nasa.gov/

❏ **NASA Observatorium**
observe.ivv.nasa.gov/

❏ **NASA Space Center**
www.jsc.nasa.gov/

❏ **National Air and Space Museum**
www.nasm.si.edu/

❏ **National Space Society**
www.nss.org/

❏ **Project Galileo**
www.jpl.nasa.gov/galileo/

❏ **Satellite Tracking**
liftoff.msfc.nasa.gov/realtime/jtrack/

❏ **Space Library**
samadhi.jpl.nasa.gov/

❏ **Space Telescope Science Institute**
www.stsci.edu//

❏ **Structure and Evolution of the Universe**
universe.gsfc.nasa.gov/

❏ **Top 20 Shoemaker-Levy Images**
www.jpl.nasa.gov/sl9/top20.html

Sports

Sports is one of the most popular categories on the Internet. This is just a tiny sample. You can surely find anything in the field of sports on the Internet

❏ **ActiveUSA**
www.activeusa.com/

❏ **All Star Sites**
www.allstarsites.com/

❏ **AllSports**
www.allsports.com/

❏ **Arena Football League**
www.arenafootball.com/

❏ **Athlete Network**
athletenetwork.com/

❏ **Baseball Time Machine**
www.exploratorium.edu/baseball/
timemachine.html

❏ **Basketball Server**
www4.nando.net/SportServer/basketball/

❏ **Coaching Science Abstracts**
www-rohan.sdsu.edu/dept/coachsci/
index.htm

❏ **College Sports News Daily**
chili.collegesportsnews.com/default.htm

❏ **College Sports Online**
www.collegesports-online.com/

❏ **Cool Running**
www.coolrunning.com/

❏ **CyberPump**
www.cyberpump.com/

❏ **Daily Racing Form**
www.drf.com/

❏ **ESPN SportsZone**
espnet.sportszone.com/

❏ **e-sports!**
www.e-sports.com/

❑ **Extreme Sports**
www.extremesports.com/

❑ **Fans Only**
www.fansonly.com/

❑ **Figure Skating Page**
frog.simplenet.com/skateweb/

❑ **Freestyle Frisbee**
www.frisbee.com/

❑ **GolfWeb**
www.golfweb.com

❑ **GoSki**
www.goski.com/

❑ **Hockey Over Time**
www.lcshockey.com/history/

❑ **Journal of Basketball Studies**
www.tsoft.net/~deano/

❑ **Monday Night Football**
espn.go.com/abcsports/mnf/

❑ **NASCAR.com**
www.nascar.com/

❑ **NBA.com**
www.nba.com/

❑ **NCAA News**
www.ncaa.org/news/

❑ **NFL.com**
www.nfl.com/

❑ **Olympic Movement**
www.olympic.org/

❑ **On Hoops**
www.onhoops.com/

❑ **Professional Sports Car Racing**
www.professionalsportscar.com/

❑ **Rollerblade**
www.rollerblade.com/

❑ **Runner's World Online**
www.runnersworld.com/

❑ **Sailing Source**
paw.com/sail/

❑ **Science of Baseball**
www.exploratorium.edu/baseball/

❑ **ScubaDuba**
www.scubaduba.com/

❑ **Skate City**
www.skatecity.com/

❑ **SkiNet**
www.iski.com/

❑ **Skydive Archive**
www.afn.org/skydive/

❑ **Snowboarding Online**
www.twsnow.com/

❑ **SnoWeb**
www.snoweb.com

❏ **SoccerNet**
soccernet.com/

❏ **Sporting News**
www.sportingnews.com/

❏ **Sports.com**
www.sports.com/

❏ **Sports Illustrated**
pathfinder.com/si/simagazine.html

❏ **Sports Illustrated for Kids**
www.sikids.com/

❏ **Stadiums and Arenas**
www.wwcd.com/stadiums.html

❏ **Surf Check**
www.surfcheck.com/

❏ **The Sports Network**
www.sportsnetwork.com/

❏ **Total Baseball**
www.totalbaseball.com/

❏ **U.S. Masters Diving**
www.n2.net/diving/

❏ **U.S. Swimming**
www.usswim.org/

❏ **USA Gymnastics Online**
www.usa-gymnastics.org/

❏ **USA National Rugby Team**
www.usa-eagles.org/

❏ **Volleyball.com**
www.volleyball.com/

❏ **Volleyball Hall of Fame**
www.volleyhall.org/

❏ **VolleyballSeek**
www.volleyballseek.com/

❏ **Water Zone**
members.aol.com/adstring/water.htm

❏ **WeightsNet**
www.weightsnet.com/

❏ **Welcome to the Pro Football Hall of Fame**
www.profootballhof.com/

❏ **Windsurfer.com**
www.windsurfer.com/

❏ **WNBA.com**
www.wnba.com/

❏ **Your League**
www.yourleague.com/

States

*Most states offer many sites, especially related
to tourism. The ones listed here are, for the most
part, the "official" sites. Some are strictly govern-
mental, but most are broader in scope.*

❏ **Alabama**
www.state.al.us/

❑ **Alaska**
www.state.ak.us/

❑ **Arizona**
www.state.az.us/

❑ **Arkansas**
www.state.ar.us/

❑ **California**
www.ca.gov/

❑ **Colorado**
www.state.co.us/

❑ **Connecticut**
www.state.ct.us/

❑ **Delaware**
www.state.de.us/

❑ **Florida**
originalflorida.org/

❑ **Georgia**
www.state.ga.us/

❑ **Hawaii**
www.hawaii.net/cgi-bin/hhp?

❑ **Idaho**
www.state.id.us/

❑ **Illinois**
www.state.il.us/

❑ **Indiana**
www.state.in.us/

❏ **Iowa**
www.state.ia.us/index.html

❏ **Kansas**
www.state.ks.us/

❏ **Kentucky**
www.state.ky.us/

❏ **Louisiana**
www.state.la.us/

❏ **Maine**
www.state.me.us/

❏ **Maryland**
www.state.md.us/

❏ **Massachusetts**
www.magnet.state.ma.us/

❏ **Michigan**
www.state.mi.us/

❏ **Minnesota**
www.state.mn.us/

❏ **Mississippi**
www.state.ms.us/

❏ **Missouri**
www.state.mo.us/

❏ **Montana**
www.state.mt.us/

❏ **Nebraska**
www.state.ne.us/

❑ **Nevada**
www.state.nv.us/

❑ **New Hampshire**
www.state.nh.us/

❑ **New Jersey**
www.state.nj.us/

❑ **New Mexico**
www.state.nm.us/

❑ **New York**
www.state.ny.us/

❑ **North Carolina**
www.state.nc.us/

❑ **North Dakota**
www.state.nd.us/

❑ **Ohio**
www.ohio.gov/

❑ **Oklahoma**
www.oklaosf.state.ok.us/

❑ **Oregon**
www.state.or.us/

❑ **Pennsylvania**
www.state.pa.us/

❑ **Rhode Island**
visitrhodeisland.com/

❑ **South Carolina**
www.state.sc.us/

❑ **South Dakota**
www.state.sd.us/

❑ **Tennessee**
www.state.tn.us/

❑ **Texas**
www.state.tx.us/

❑ **Utah**
www.state.ut.us/

❑ **Vermont**
www.state.vt.us/

❑ **Virginia**
www.state.va.us/

❑ **Washington**
access.wa.gov/

❑ **West Virginia**
www.state.wv.us/

❑ **Wisconsin**
www.state.wi.us/

❑ **Wyoming**
www.state.wy.us/

Statistics

There's some pretty interesting stuff here. Statistics, as presented to the public, definitely are not boring.

❑ **Consumer Price Indexes**
stats.bls.gov/cpihome.htm

❑ **Criminal Justice Statistics**
www.albany.edu/sourcebook/

❑ **Demography and Population Studies**
coombs.anu.edu.au/ResFacilities/
DemographyPage.html

❑ **Fedstats**
www.fedstats.gov/

❑ **GlobalStatistics**
www.stats.demon.nl/

❑ **Journal of Statistics Education**
www2.ncsu.edu/ncsu/pams/stat/info/jse/
homepage.html

❑ **Justice Statistics**
www.ojp.usdoj.gov/bjs/

❑ **Labor Statistics**
stats.bls.gov

❑ **National Highway Traffic Safety**
www.nhtsa.dot.gov/

❑ **Statistical Methodology**
www.bts.gov/fcsm/

❑ **Statistics Every Writer Should Know**
nilesonline.com/stats/

❑ **StatLib Index**
temper.stat.cmu.edu/

❑ **Stat-USA**
www.stat-usa.gov/

❑ **Transportation Statistics**
www.bts.gov/

❑ **U.S. Census Bureau**
www.census.gov/

❏ **World Population**
sunsite.unc.edu/lunarbin/worldpop

Streaming

Hear it and see it, directly from the Internet.

❏ **15 Minutes**
www.zeldman.com/15/

❏ **ChannelSeek**
channelseek.com/

❏ **Court TV**
www.courttv.com/video/

❏ **Internet Radio Stations**
radiotower.com/internetradio/liveaudio.asp

❏ **Living SkiMaps**
www.skimaps.com/Video/

❏ **PowerPoint Streaming**
www.powerpointstreaming.com/

❏ **Rolling Stone Radio**
www.rsradio.com/home/

❏ **Streaming Independent Music and Video**
www.nolabel.com/index.html

❏ **Streaming Media**
www.calstatela.edu/ats/real/develop/

❏ **Streaming Media World**
streamingmediaworld.com/

Taxes

There may be something helpful here for individuals or businesses.

❏ **Estate and Gift Tax Law**
www.law.cornell.edu/topics/estate_gift_tax.html

❏ **Flat Tax Home Page**
flattax.house.gov/

❏ **Green Taxes Report**
www.ilsr.org/ecotax/greentax.html

❏ **IRS Tax Terms**
www.irs.ustreas.gov/prod/taxi/taxterms.html

❏ **Nolo's Legal Encyclopedia—Tax Problems**
www.nolo.com/ChunkTAX/TAX.index.html

❏ **Sports, Jobs, and Taxes**
www.brook.edu/pub/review/summer97/noll.htm

❏ **Tax Analysts Online**
www.tax.org/

❏ **Tax Freedom Institute**
www.taxhelponline.com/tfihome.htm

❏ **Tax Prophet**
www.taxprophet.com/

❏ **Tax Resources**
www.taxresources.com/

❏ **Tax Season Survival Kit**
freedom.house.gov/survival/

❏ **Tax Tables**
www.irs.ustreas.gov/prod/ind_info/tax_
tables/index.html

❏ **Tax Web**
www.taxweb.com/

❏ **Tax World**
www.taxworld.org/

❏ **Taxes FAQ**
www.landfield.com/faqs/taxes-faq/part1/

❏ **TaxHelpOnline**
www.taxhelponline.com/

❏ **TaxLinks**
www.taxlinks.com/

❏ **U.S. Tax Code Online**
www.fourmilab.ch/ustax/ustax.html

Techie Company Sites

*Makers of hardware and software—their sites
better be cool, right? Also, if you are looking for a
job in the computer field, these sites often
describe openings and solicit applications.*

❏ **3COM**
www.3com.com/

❏ **Adaptec**
www.adaptec.com/

❏ **Adobe Systems**
www.adobe.com/

❏ **America Online**
www.aol.com/

❏ **American Micro Devices**
www.amd.com/

❏ **Apple**
www.apple.com

❏ **Autodesk**
www.autodesk.com

❏ **Banyan**
www.banyan.com

❏ **Borland**
www.borland.com/

❏ **Brightpoint**
www.brightpoint.com/static/global/global.htm

❏ **Broderbund**
www.broderbund.com/

❏ **Cisco**
www.cisco.com/

❏ **Citrix Systems**
www.citrix.com/

❏ **Compaq**
www.compaq.com/

❏ **Computer Associates**
www.cai.com/

❏ **Corel**
www.corel.com/

❑ **Cyrix**
www.cyrix.com

❑ **Dell**
www.dell.com/

❑ **DoubleClick**
www.doubleclick.net

❑ **Firefly**
www.firefly.com/

❑ **Gateway 2000**
www.gw2k.com/

❑ **Hewlett-Packard**
www.hp.com/

❑ **Inktomi**
www.inktomi.com/

❑ **Intel**
www.intel.com/

❑ **Iomega**
www.iomega.com/

❑ **Lucent**
www.lucent.com

❑ **Micron**
www.micron.com/

❑ **Microsoft**
www.microsoft.com/

❑ **Morning Star Technologies**
www.morningstar.com/

❑ **Motorola**
www.mot.com/

❑ **National Semiconductor**
www.national.com/

❑ **NEC**
www.nec.com

❑ **NetObjects**
www.netobjects.com

❑ **Pixar**
www.pixar.com/

❑ **Quantum**
www.quantum.com/

❑ **SAP**
www.sap.com/

❑ **Shiva**
www.shiva.com

❑ **Sierra**
www.sierra.com/

❑ **Sun Microsystems**
www.sun.com/

❑ **Symantec**
www.symantec.com/

❑ **Texas Instrument**
www.ti.com/

❑ **Trilogy**
www.trilogy.com/

❑ **Veritas**
www.veritas.com

❑ **Vitesse**
www.vitesse.com/

❑ **Wind River**
www.windriver.com/

Television

The premiere shows and the major networks have their own sites. The other sites include listings, reviews, and historical perspectives.

❑ **Academy of Television Arts and Sciences**
www.emmys.org/

❑ **A&3**
www.aande.com/

❑ **Ad Critic**
www.adcritic.com/

❑ **American Movie Classics**
www.amctv.com/

❑ **Antiques Roadshow**
www.pbs.org/wgbh/pages/roadshow/
home.html

❑ **Austin Cyber Limits**
www.pbs.org/kiru/austin

❑ **Best Bits of Britcom**
britcom.interspeed.net/

❑ **Biography**
www.biography.com/

❏ **CBS.com**
www.cbs.com/

❏ **CNN Interactive**
www.cnn.com/

❏ **Computer Chronicles**
www.cmptv.com/computerchronicles/

❏ **Court TV Famous Cases**
www.courttv.com/famous/

❏ **C-SPAN**
www.c-span.org/

❏ **Discovery Channel**
www.discovery.com/

❏ **E! Online**
www.eonline.com/

❏ **Free TV Tickets**
www.tvtix.com/

❏ **Frontline**
www2.pbs.org/wgbh/pages/frontline/

❏ **Gist**
www.thegist.com/

❏ **Golden Age of Television**
www.aentv.com/home/golden/goldtv.htm

❏ **History Channel**
www.historychannel.com/

❏ **Infomercial Index**
www.magickeys.com/infomercials/

❏ **Lifetime Online**
www.lifetimetv.com/

❑ **MSNBC**
www.msnbc.com/

❑ **NBC.com**
www.nbc.com/

❑ **Nielsen Media Research**
www.nielsenmedia.com/

❑ **NOVA Online**
www.pbs.org/wgbh/nova/

❑ **Parents Television Council**
www.parentstv.org/

❑ **PBS Online**
www.pbs.org/

❑ **Primetime Review**
www.primetimereview.com/

❑ **Quizsite**
www.quizsite.com

❑ **RockOnTV**
www.rockontv.com

❑ **Soap Opera Central**
www.amcpages.com/soapcentral/

❑ **The Museum of Television & Radio**
www.mtr.org/

❑ **TV Barn**
www.tvbarn.com/

❑ **TV Collectibles**
www.jimtvc.com/

❑ **TV Guide**
www.tvguide.com/

❏ **TV News Archive**
tvnews.vanderbilt.edu/

❏ **TV-Ultra**
www.tvultra.com/

❏ **Ultimate TV**
www.ultimatetv.com/

❏ **Unsolved Mysteries**
www.unsolved.com/missing.html

❏ **Yesterdayland**
www.yesterdayland.com/

Testing

If you need to take any kind of test for academic admission, help is as close as your computer. This list includes the official sites of the test makers and several for folks who would like to help you, usually for a fee.

❏ **ACT Assessment**
www.act.org

❏ **Berkeley Review MCAT Prep**
www.berkeley-review.com/

❏ **College Board Online**
www.collegeboard.org/

❏ **College PowerPrep**
www.powerprep.com/

❏ **Columbia Review MCAT Prep**
www.columbiareview.com/

❏ **Educational Testing Service Network**
www.ets.org/

❏ **GMAT Coaching**
www.angelfire.com/biz/gmatcoaching/
gmat.html

❏ **GoCollege**
www.gocollege.com/

❏ **GRE Test Prep**
4testprep.com/gre/

❏ **Kaplan: Test Yourself**
www.kaplan.com/library/testself.html

❏ **Law School Admission Council LSAT**
www.lsac.org/

❏ **Lighthouse Review**
www.lighthousereview.com/

❏ **LSAT Intelligent Solutions**
www.gate.net/~tutor/

Theatre

What's on, who's playing, what's good, what isn't—It's all here.

❏ **American Association of Community Theatre**
www.aact.org/

❏ **American Cabaret Theatre**
www.americancabarettheatre.com/Theatre/
about.html

❏ **American Repertory Theatre**
www.amrep.org/

❏ **American Theater Web**
www.americantheaterweb.com/

❏ **Broadway Theater Online**
www.broadwaytheater.com/

❏ **Broadway Theatre Archive**
www.tbta.com/home.html

❏ **Carnegie Hall**
www.carnegiehall.org/

❏ **Costume Source**
www.milieux.com/costume/source.html

❏ **ExxonMobil Masterpiece Theatre**
www.pbs.org/wgbh/masterpiece/

❏ **Family Theater Guide**
nyctourist.com/bway_familyguide.htm

❏ **Glossary of Technical Theatre Terms**
www.ex.ac.uk/drama/tech/glossary.html

❏ **History of Costumes**
www.siue.edu/COSTUMES/history.html

❏ **Improv Page**
sunee.uwaterloo.ca/~broehl/improv/

❏ **London Theatre Guide**
www.londontheatre.co.uk/

❏ **Musicals Net**
musicals.net/

❏ **On Broadway**
artsnet.heinz.cmu.edu/OnBroadway/

❏ **Playbill**
www1.playbill.com/playbill/

❏ **Shakespeare and the Globe**
starone.com/actorsweb/

❏ **Stage Directions Magazine**
www.stage-directions.com/

❏ **Talkin' Broadway**
www.talkinbroadway.com/

❏ **The Internet Theatre Database**
www.theatredb.com/

❏ **Tony Awards**
www.tonys.org/

❏ **Welcome to Ford's Theatre**
www.fordstheatre.org/

❏ **What's on Stage**
www.whatsonstage.com/

Travel Destinations and Adventures

As is so often true in regard to the Internet, this list is just a small sample. If you have a specific distination in mind, you can surely find several sites that tell you anything you would like to know.

❏ **10 Downing Street**
www.number-10.gov.uk/

❏ **360 alaska**
www.360alaska.com/index.htm

❏ **Adventure Destinations**
www.adventuredestinations.com/

❏ **Air Courier Travel**
www.jps.net/nickstas/

❏ **Alaska Ferries**
www.akms.com/ferry/

❏ **America's Roof**
www.americasroof.com/

❏ **Backroads Traveler**
www.backroads.com/

❏ **Balloons Over New England**
www.pbpub.com/bal1.htm

❏ **Beaches and Islands**
travel.epicurious.com/traveler/great_escapes/
great_escapes.html

❏ **Bellringing at Canterbury Cathedral**
web.ukonline.co.uk/Members/mark.gilham/
cathedral/index.htm

❏ **Best Beaches**
www.petrix.com/beaches/

❏ **Betsy Ross House**
www.libertynet.org/iha/betsy/

❏ **Bird Treks**
www.birdtreks.com/

❏ **Botanical Gardens**
www.helsinki.fi/kmus/botgard.html

❏ **Covered Bridges**
william-king.www.drexel.edu/top/bridge/
CB1.html

❏ **Crazy Horse**
www.crazyhorse.org/

❏ **EarthWise Journeys**
www.teleport.com/~earthwyz/index.htm

❏ **European Walking Tours**
www.gorp.com/est/

❏ **Fall in Pennsylvania**
www.fallinpa.com/

❏ **Freighter Cruises**
www.freighterworld.com/

❏ **Ghost Towns**
www.cultimedia.ch/ghosttowns/

❏ **Graceland**
www.elvis-presley.com/

❏ **Hamptons**
www.thehamptons.com/

❏ **Hawaii**
www.visit.hawaii.org/

❏ **Hearst Castle**
www.hearstcastle.org/

❏ **Hidden America**
www.hiddenamerica.com/

❑ **Hidden Trails**
www.hiddentrails.com/

❑ **Hostel Links**
www.ping.be/~ping0420/

❑ **Learning Vacations**
www.learningvacations.com/

❑ **Legendary Lighthouses**
www.pbs.org/legendarylighthouses/

❑ **Lift Hill**
www.lifthill.com/

❑ **Mardi Gras**
usacitylink.com/mardigr/default.html

❑ **Montana High Country Cattle Drive**
www.iigi.com/os/montana/cattledr/
cattledr.htm

❑ **Monterey Bay Aqaurium**
www.mbayaq.org/

❑ **Moss Springs Packing**
www.iigi.com/os/oregon/moss/vacation.htm

❑ **Mount Rushmore**
www.libertynet.org/iha/betsy/

❑ **Mysterious Places**
mysteriousplaces.com/

❑ **National Register of Historic Places**
www.cr.nps.gov/nr/

❑ **Nature Tours**
naturetour.com/

❏ **New England Winding Roads**
miraclemile.com/windingroads/

❏ **OK Corral**
www.ok-corral.com/

❏ **Old Sturbridge Village**
www.osv.org/

❏ **OnSafari**
www.onsafari.com/

❏ **Orient Express**
www.orient-expresstrains.com/

❏ **Participate in Archeology**
www.cr.nps.gov/aad/particip.htm

❏ **Public Aquariums**
www.actwin.com/fish/public.cgi

❏ **Ranch Vacations**
www.travelsource.com/ranches/

❏ **Ranchweb**
www.ranchweb.com/

❏ **Rollercoasters**
www.rollercoaster.com/

❏ **Roman Monuments**
www.roma2000.it/zmonum2.
html#Monumenti

❏ **Scenic Byways**
www.byways.org/

❏ **South Georgia Island**
www.pbs.org/edens/southgeorgia/

❑ South Pole Adventure
www.southpole.com/

❑ Spa Finder
www.spafinders.com/

❑ Swimmers Guide
lornet.com/~SGOL/

❑ Taj Mahal
www.angelfire.com/in/myindia/
tajmahal.html

❑ The Ice
www.io.com/~pml/welcome.html

❑ Travel @ the Speed of Light
vanbc.wimsey.com/~ayoung/travel.shtml

❑ Ventura Expeditions
www.subnet.co.uk/ventura/

❑ Wall Drug
www.state.sd.us/state/executive/tourism/
adds/walldrug.htm

❑ Whale Watching
www.physics.helsinki.fi.whale/

❑ Wild-Eyed Alaska
www.hhmi.org/alaska/

❑ World Federation of Great Towers
www.great-towers.com/

❑ World Wide Events
www.events.com/

❏ **World's Largest Roadside Attractions**
www.infomagic.com/~martince/index.htm

Travel Planning Information

Anything related to travel, from checking out an obscure location to making airline reservations, can be found on the Internet.

❏ **1000 Tips 4 Trips**
www.tips4trips.com/Tips/plantips

❏ **Accessible Jouneys**
www.disabilitytravel.com/

❏ **Air Travel Complaints**
www.airtravelcomplaints.com/

❏ **Airline Toll-Free Numbers**
www.princeton.edu/Main/air800.html

❏ **AlaskaOne.com**
www.alaskaone.com/

❏ **All by Word of Mouse**
wordofmouse.com/

❏ **All Hotels on the Web**
www.all-hotels.com/

❏ **American Sightseeing International**
www.sightseeing.com/

❏ **American Student Travel**
www.astravel.com/

❏ **Amtrak**
www.amtrak.com/

❑ **Australia Travel Company**
www.australian.com/

❑ **BC Ferries**
www.bcferries.bc.ca/travel_planning.html

❑ **Bed and Breakfast Inns of North America**
cimarron.net/

❑ **CitySearch**
www.citysearch.com/

❑ **Civilized Explorer**
www.cieux.com/

❑ **Cruise Ship Opinion**
www.cruiseopinion.com/

❑ **Discount Airfares**
www.aesu.com/

❑ **Escape Artist**
www.escapeartist.com/

❑ **Escapees RV Club**
www.channel1.com/users/escapees/

❑ **European Railway Server**
mercurio.iet.unipi.it/home.html

❑ **Expedia Travel**
www.expedia.com/

❑ **Fodors.com**
www.fodors.com/

❑ **Fodor's NetTravel**
www.ypn.com/living/travel/

❑ **Foreign Languages for Travelers**
www.travlang.com/languages/

❏ **Frommer's Outspoken Encyclopedia of Travel**
www.frommers.com/

❏ **gaytravel.com**
www.gay-travel.com/

❏ **Get Cruising**
www.getcruising.com/

❏ **Greyhound Lines, Inc**
www.greyhound.com/travel/

❏ **Guatemala Travel**
www.guatemalatravel.com/

❏ **Guide to Bed and Breakfast Inns**
www.ultranet.com/biz/inns/

❏ **Guide to Sleeping in Airports**
www3.sympatico.ca/donna.mcsherry/
airports.htm

❏ **Hostels of Europe**
www.hostelseurope.com/

❏ **Hotel Discounts**
www.hoteldiscount.com/

❏ **How to See the World**
www.artoftravel.com/index.html

❏ **Innkeeper**
www.theinnkeeper.com/

❏ **Insiders' Guides**
www.insiders.com/

❏ **International Vacation Homes**
www.ivacation.com/

❑ **Lonely Planet**
www.lonelyplanet.com/

❑ **Microsoft Expedia**
www.expedia.msn.com

❑ **National Travel Exchange**
www.travelx.com/

❑ **O Solo Mio**
www.osolomio.com/

❑ **Opinionated Traveler**
www.opinionatedtraveler.com/

❑ **Passenger Rights**
www.passengerrights.com/

❑ **Passport Services**
travel.state.gov/passport_services.html

❑ **Priceline**
www.priceline.com/

❑ **Rec.Travel Library**
www.Travel-Library.com/

❑ **Roadside America**
www.roadsideamerica.com/index.html

❑ **Roswell Travel Planning**
gosouthwest.about.com/cs/roswell4/
?rnk=r7&terms=Roswell

❑ **Rough Guides**
www.hotwired.com/rough/

❑ **See the World on $25 a Day**
www.artoftravel.com/

❑ **Tahiti Travel**
www.tahitiexperts.com/tahiti-travel-dir45.htm

❑ **TheTrip**
www.thetrip.com/

❑ **Third World Traveler**
www.thirdworldtraveler.com/

❑ **Travel Connection**
www.travelxn.com/

❑ **TravelFile**
tfsrvr.travelfile.com/

❑ **Travelocity**
www.travelocity.com/

❑ **Travel Insurance**
www.wemark.com/nuim.html

❑ **Travel Planning for People with Handicaps**
sussex.njstatelib.org/njlib/bhtravel.htm

❑ **Travelzoo**
www.travelzoo.com/

❑ **TRIP.com**
www.thetrip.com/home/0,1311,1-1,00.html

❑ **U.S State Home Pages**
www.globalcomputing.com/states.html

❑ **U.S. State Department Travel Warnings**
www.stolaf.edu/network/travel-advisories.
html

❑ **USA CityLink**
banzai.neosoft.com/citylink/

❏ **United States of America Page**
sunsite.unc.edu/usa/usahome.html

❏ **Vacation Rental Source**
www.vrsource.com/

❏ **Virtual Tourist**
www.vtourist.com/webmap/

❏ **Web Travel Review**
photo.net/webtravel/

❏ **WebFlyer**
www.webflyer.com/Worldwide Brochures

❏ **World's Most Dangerous Places**
www.fieldingtravel.com/dr/index.htm

Travel—Restaurant Guides

Around the world or down the street—You have to eat somewhere.

❏ **ActiveDiner**
www.activediner.com/HomePage.cfm

❏ **Celebrity Fare**
pathfinder.com/people/celebrityfare/

❏ **Chicago Area Restaurant Guides**
jean.nu/chicago/restaurants.html

❏ **Choose a City**
www.zagat.com/

❏ **Chowhound**
www.chowhound.com/

❏ **Cuisine.Net**
www.dinnerandamovie.com/

❏ **Dine.com**
www.dine.com/

❏ **Diner City**
www.dinercity.com/

❏ **Diners' Grapevine World Restaurant Guide**
www.dinersgrapevine.com/

❏ **Dinner and a Movie**
www.dinnerandamovie.com/

❏ **Eat Here**
www.eathere.com

❏ **Eat in Germany**
www.eat-germany.net/

❏ **EatNet**
www.eatnet.com/

❏ **Fodor's Restaurant Index**
www.fodors.com/ri.cgi

❏ **Kosher Restaurant Database**
shamash.org/kosher/

❏ **Restaurant Guides, New York City**
www.joseph-memphis.com/dining/
ny-rest.htm

❏ **Restaurant Row**
www.restaurantrow.com/

❏ **Restaurants New York City**
www.newyorkmall.com/res-restlinks.html

❑ **Savvy Diner Restaurant Guide**
www.savvydiner.com/

❑ **Sushi World Guide**
www.sushi.infogate.de/

❑ **The Kitchen Link**
www.kitchenlink.com/comm.html

❑ **Top100**
www.top100.com.au/aust/food_and_wine/
restaurant_guides/

❑ **U.K. Restaurant Guides**
www.shophunters.co.uk/ukrestaurants.html

❑ **Unione Ristoranti del Buon Ricordo**
www.pantarei.it/buonricordo/

❑ **U.S. Dining Guide**
shamash.org/kosher/

❑ **VegEats!**
www.vegeats.com/restaurants/

❑ **Washington, D.C., Restaurants**
www.washingtonian.com/dining/

❑ **www.fat-guy.com**
www.shaw-review.com/

Travel—Virtual Tours

Go anywhere but stay where you are. These sites give the feeling of the trip without having to pack a bag.

❑ **Amsterdam**
www.channels.nl/

❏ **Amsterdam Virtual Tour**
www.channels.nl/

❏ **Ancient Sites Tours**
www.ancientsites.com/as/home/features/
astours.html

❏ **Animal Kingdom Virtual Tour**
members.tripod.com/adm/popup/roadmap.
shtml

❏ **Belize Virtual Tour**
www.travelbelize.org/guide/guidehp.html

❏ **Boeing Virtual Tour**
www.boeing.com/companyoffices/gallery/
video/

❏ **Budapest Virtual Tour**
www.budapest.com/

❏ **Castles on the Web**
www.castlesontheweb.com/

❏ **Civil War Virtual Battlefield Tours**
www.geocities.com/Pentagon/Bunker/8757/
cwvirtual.html

❏ **Gothic Cathedrals**
www.newyorkcarver.com/cathedrallinks.htm

❏ **Great Wall of China Virtual Tour**
www.chinavista.com/travel/greatwall/
greatwall.html

❏ **Heart of San Antonio**
heartofsanantonio.com/tourcity/index.asp

❏ **Jerusalem Virtual Tour**
www.md.huji.ac.il/vjt/

❏ **Jordanian Virtual Tours**
www.acsamman.edu.jo/~ms/crusades/
virtual.html

❏ **Lizzie Borden House Virtual Tour**
www.halfmoon.org/borden/

❏ **Maui Virtual Tours**
maui.unclewebster.com/tours/

❏ **Mendenhall Glacier Virtual Tour**
www.snowcrest.net/geography/field/
mendenhall/index.html

❏ **Miami Virtual Tour**
www.miamivr.com/

❏ **Morocco**
www.maghreb.net/countries/morocco/

❏ **Museums and Virtual Tours**
www.intradatechnologies.com/Links/
student/museumtours.htm

❏ **National Civil Rights Museum
Virtual Tour**
www.mecca.org/~crights/cyber.html

❏ **New Zealand Virtual Tour**
www.nz.com/tour/

❏ **Norfolk Island Virtual Tour**
www.nz.com/tour/

❏ **Parks Canada Virtual Tours**
parkscanada.pch.gc.ca/thesite/virtual_e.cfm

❏ **Pompeii Forum Project**
jefferson.village.virginia.edu/ponpeii/
page-1.html

❏ **Revolutionary War Virtual Battlefield Tours**
www.geocities.com/Pentagon/Bunker/8757/
revvirtual.html

❏ **San Diego Model Railroad Virtual Tour**
www.globalinfo.com/noncomm/SDMRM/
sdmrm.html

❏ **Sistine Chapel**
www.christusrex.org/www1/sistine/
0-Tour.html

❏ **Sugar Loaf Virtual Tour**
www.bondinho.com.br/

❏ **Swissôtel**
www.swissotel.com/virtual-tour.html

❏ **Torquay**
www.halien.com/tour/Torquay/intro.htm

❏ **Tower of London Virtual Tour**
www.toweroflondontour.com/

❏ **Travel Alaska**
www.travelalaska.com/tours/
rightframetours2.html

❏ **Travel Australia**
www.travelau.com.au/

❏ **Venice Virtual Tour**
www.virtualvenice.com/

❑ **Virtual Field Trips**
www.field-guides.com/

❑ **Virtual Road Trip**
virtualroadtrip.com/

❑ **Virtual Tours of Astronomical Observatories**
tdc-www.harvard.edu/mthopkins/
obstours.html

❑ **Yemen Virtual Tour**
www.yemennet.com/tour/yemen.thm

Useful Stuff

And we mean really useful. No esoteric computer stuff, just the info we need on occasion.

❑ **800 Phone Numbers**
www.inter800.com/

❑ **Ability Utility**
www.learn2.com/

❑ **Area Code Lookup**
www.555-1212.com/ACLOOKUP.HTML

❑ **Convert It!**
www.microimg.com/science/

❑ **Credit Score Secrets**
creditscoring.com/

❑ **Disabilities Information Resources**
www.dinf.org/

❑ **Electronic Ticket Exchange**
www.tixs.com/

❏ **Freedom of Information Request**
www.rcfp.org/foi_lett.html

❏ **How Far Is It?**
www.indo.com/distance/

❏ **How Stuff Works**
www.howstuffworks.com/

❏ **Lost and Found**
www.lost-and-found.com/lostfound.html

❏ **Megaconverter**
www.megaconverter.com/

❏ **New York Subway Instruction Page**
www.juvenilemedia/com/subway/

❏ **PostagePlus**
www.postageplus.com

❏ **Reverse Telephone Directory**
www.anywho.com/telq.html

❏ **Speedtrap Registry**
www.speedtrap.com/speedtrap/

❏ **Traffic Waves**
www.eskimo.com/~billb/amateur/traffic/
traffic1.html

❏ **Useful Site of the Day**
www.zdnet.com/yil/content/depts/useful/
useful.html

❏ **VCR Repair**
www.fixer.com

❏ **Wacky Uses**
www.wackyuses.com/

❏ **World Clock**
www.stud.unit.no/USERBIN/steffent/
verdensur.pl

❏ **Zip Code Lookup**
www.usps.gov/ncsc/

Virtual Community

Each of these sites have multiple and varied offerings. But the main attraction is some sort of user connection, usually in the form of live chat.

❏ **Asian Avenue**
www.communityconnect.com/AsianAvenue.
html

❏ **Biz Women**
www.bizwomen.com/

❏ **Black Voices**
www.blackvoices.com/

❏ **Café de Paris**
paris-anglo.com/café/

❏ **Caribbean City**
www.caribbeancity.com/

❏ **ChatPlanet**
www.chatplanet.com

❏ **Cloud City**
www.angelfire.com/ny/acloud/

❏ **CNN Community Discussion**
cnn.com/discussion/

❏ **Crafters Network**
crafters.net/

❏ **Cybercafes Worldwide**
www.netcafeguide.com/

❏ **Delphi Forum**
www.delphi.com/

❏ **Electric Minds**
www.minds.com/

❏ **FolksOnline**
www.folksonline.com/

❏ **Food Ingredients Online**
www.foodingredientsonline.com/

❏ **Ivillage**
www.ivillage.com/

❏ **LatinoLink**
www.latinolink.com/

❏ **LostWorlds**
www.lost-worlds.com/

❏ **Rain Web**
www.rain.org

❏ **Reality Check**
www.realitycheck.com/

❏ **Serendip**
serendip.brynmawr.edu/

❏ **Substance Abuse Training**
www3.umassd.edu/addiction/

❏ **Talk City**
www.talkcity.com/

❑ **Talkz.com**
www.talkz.com/

❑ **Teen.com**
www.teen.com/

❑ **The Well**
www.well.com/

❑ **Weight Loss Support**
camden-www.rutgers.edu/~wood/445/
hind.html

❑ **WheelchairNet**
www.wheelchairnet.org/

❑ **Whole Earth**
www.wholeearthmag.com/ArticleBin/269.html

❑ **World Village**
www.worldvillage.com/

❑ **Worlds Away**
www.worldsaway.com/

❑ **Y'all**
www.accessatlanta.com/global/local/yall/

Volunteer Vacations

*Not sure about a two-year commitment to the
Peace Corps? Try a volunteer vacation first.*

❑ **4Volunteer**
www.crossculturalsolutions.org/prjectindia/
vlntr_abrd.html

❑ **Amizade Volunteer Vacations**
amizade.org/programs.htm

❏ **Earth-Friendly Living**
www.enn.com/enn-features-archive/1999/
06/061799/earthwatch_3745.asp

❏ **Earthwatch Institute**
www.earthwatch.org/

❏ **EarthWise Journeys**
www.teleport.com/~earthwyz/volunt.htm

❏ **Fielding's DangerFinder**
www.comebackalive.com/df/advcalls/
voltrvac.htm

❏ **Mano Amiga**
www.manoamiga.net/

❏ **Other Adventures: Volunteer Vacations**
www.mountwashingtonvalley.com/
top-of-the-world/other4.html

❏ **Sousson Foundation**
www.sousson.org/students.html

❏ **Spartan Travel, Inc.**
www.spartantravel.com/page.cfm/194/

❏ **Start Thinking About a Volunteer Vacation**
www.ihad.org/

❏ **Survival Vacations**
www.monroe.lib.in.us/teens/
summer99teens/survival.html

❏ **Vagabunda!**
www.vagabunda.com/shopping/gs01032000.
html

❏ Volunteer Abroad
www.crossculturalsolutions.org/
projectindia/vlntr_abrd.html

Weather

If you need to know now, the Internet is your fastest and most complete weather source.

❏ Accuweather
www.accuweather.com/

❏ BBC Weather Centre
www.bbc.co.uk/weather/

❏ Bureau of Meteorology
www.bom.gov.au/

❏ CNN Weather
www.cnn.com/WEATHER/index.html

❏ Current Atlantic Tropical Storms
www.solar.ifa.hawaii.edu/Tropical/Gif/
atl.latest.gif

❏ EarthWatch Weather on Demand
www.earthwatch.com/

❏ Hurricane Hunters
www.hurricanehunters.com/welcome.htm

❏ Intellicast
www.intellicast.com/

❏ Interactive Weather Information Network
iwin.nws.noaa.gov/iwin/main.html

❏ Marine Weather
www.marineweather.com/

❑ **National Climatic Data Center**
www.ncdc.noaa.gov/

❑ **National Hurricane Center**
www.nhc.noaa.gov/iwin/

❑ **National Weather Service**
www.nws.noaa.gov/

❑ **National Warnings Area**
iwin.nws.noaa.gov/iwin/nationalwarnings.
html

❑ **Natural Disaster Reference Database**
ltpwww.gsfc.nasa.gov/ndrd/

❑ **The Weather Network**
www.theweathernetwork.com/

❑ **Tropical Storm Watch**
www.fema.gov/fema/trop.htm

❑ **Twister Chasers**
www.indirect.com/www/storm5/
tchomepage.html

❑ **Unisys Weather**
weather.unisys.com

❑ **Weather**
www.weathersite.com/

❑ **Weather Advisory**
weather.terrapin.com/

❑ **Weather and Climate Image maps**
grads.iges.org/pix/head.html

❑ **Weather by E-Mail**
www.webbers.com/weather/

❑ **Weather24**
www.weather24.com/

Weddings

Surely you would not plan your wedding on your own, not when so many people on the Internet want to help.

❑ **Affectionately Yours**
www.affectionately-yours.com/

❑ **Hawaiian Island Weddings**
www.maui.net/~weddings/

❑ **Jasmine Bridal**
www.jasminebridal.com/

❑ **My Wedding Companion**
users.southeast.net/~fivestar/

❑ **New York City Weddings**
www.nycityweddings.com/

❑ **Our Special Day**
www.ourspecialday.com/

❑ **Today's Bride**
www.todaysbride.com/

❑ **Town and Country Wedding Registry**
tncweddings.com/index.html

❑ **Traditional Scottish Weddings**
www.smo.uhi.ac.uk/~craig/weddings.html

❑ **Ultimate Internet Wedding Guide**
www.ultimatewedding.com/

❑ **Vegetarian Weddings**
vegetarian.miningco.com/library/weekly/
aa060198.htm

❑ **WayCool Weddings Every Week**
www.waycoolweddings.com/

❑ **Wedding Announcement**
www.weddingcircle.com/announce/

❑ **Wedding Channel**
www.weddingchannel.com/go/Gateway/
WeddingChannel/Intro/

❑ **Wedding Network**
www.weddingnetwork.com/

❑ **Weddings Galore!**
www.weddingsgalore.com/

❑ **Weddings Online**
weddings-online.com/

❑ **WedNet**
www.wednet.com/

❑ **White Hot Weddings**
www.bridal-links.com/

Worldly

*Take a look around the globe, and don't worry if
you speak only English.*

❑ **About Calcutta**
www.gl.umbc.edu/~achatt1/calcutta.html

❑ **Africa Online**
www.africaonline.com/

❏ **AfriCam**
www.africam.com/

❏ **Alive! Global Network**
www.alincom.com/

❏ **ArabNet**
www.arab.net/

❏ **Arctic Circle**
www.lib.uconn.edu/ArcticCircle/

❏ **AskAsia**
www.askasia.org/

❏ **Aussie Index**
www.aussie.com.au/

❏ **Bali Online**
www.indo.com/

❏ **Bangkok Post**
www.bangkokpost.net/

❏ **Blue Window**
www.bluewin.ch/index_e.html

❏ **British Monarchy**
www.royal.gov.uk/

❏ **Calgary Explorer**
www.calexplorer.com/

❏ **Canadiana**
www.cs.cmu.edu/Unofficial/Canadiana/
README.html

❏ **Caribbean Online**
www.webcom.com/earleltd/welcome.html

❏ **Carrefour International**
www.carrefour.net/

❏ **Chateau de Versailles**
www.chateauversailles.fr/

❏ **CiberCentro**
www.cibercentro.com/

❏ **Czech Info Center**
www.muselik.com/czech/frame.html

❏ **Down Under**
www.south-pacific.com/travel-zine/

❏ **Easter Island**
www.netaxs.com/~trance/rapanui.html

❏ **Ellada**
www.ellada.com/

❏ **European Roof**
www.inch.com/~dipper/europe.html

❏ **Face of Russia**
www.pbs.org/weta/faceofrussia/

❏ **Fireball Express Suche**
www.fireball.de/

❏ **France Vision**
www.francevision.com/index.htm

❏ **Global Grocery List Project**
www.landmark-project.com/ggl.html

❏ **Hong Kong**
www.hongkong.org/

❑ **International Real Estate Directory**
www.ired.com/

❑ **Italia Online**
www.iol.it/

❑ **Japan, My Japan!**
lang.nagoya-u.ac.jp/~matsuoka/Japan.html

❑ **Kiwi Web**
www.chemistry.co.nz/

❑ **La France**
www.urec.cnrs.fr/annuaire/

❑ **Laurentians**
www.ietc.ca/index.htm

❑ **Les Chroniques de Cybérie**
www.cyberie.qc.ca/chronik/

❑ **Les Pages de Paris**
www.paris.org/

❑ **Living Abroad**
www.livingabroad.com/

❑ **Loch Ness Monster**
www.pgs.org/wgbh/nova/lochness/

❑ **Mexico**
mexico.udg.mx/

❑ **Poesie Francaise**
www.webnet.fr/poesie/

❑ **St.Petersburg (Russia)**
www.spb.ru/russian/

❏ **Stockholm**
www.stockholm.se/

❏ **Strasbourg**
www.sdv.fr/strasbourg/

❏ **United Nations**
www.un.org/

❏ **Visit Your Favorite Country**
www.countries.com/

❏ **World Communities**
www.einet.net/galaxy/Community/
World-Communities.html

❏ **World Hello Day**
www.worldhelloday.org/

❏ **World's Living Guide**
www.timeout.co.uk/

❏ **Worldwide Holidays and Festivals**
www.holidayfestival.com/

❏ **Your Nation**
www.your-nation.com/

❏ **Yuan Ming Yuan**
www.cs.ubc.ca/spider/wang/

❏ **Yupi**
www.yupi.com/